About the author

John Simpson has been a keen student of steam engines for over seventy years, part of an eventful career that includes photography, gliding, and scientific research. At Cambridge University in the 1930s he was President of the Railway Club, and it was during this time that he embarked on a series of expeditions to small independent railways. During World War II he worked with the Friends Ambulance Unit in China, and there he was able to photograph steam engines on the metre gauge railway near Kunming. Returning to England, he first taught physics, and then had a long spell at the Department of Applied Mathematics and Theoretical Physics at Cambridge where he wrote over fifty scientific papers. Having recently completed a successful book on Manning Wardle locomotives, he decided to convert his youthful diaries and maps into a second book of railway history.

Light Railways Explored

A Photographic Diary
1931 - 38

John E. Simpson

Ross-Evans

British Library Cataloguing in Publication Data

Simpson, John E
Light Railways Explored: A Photographic Diary 1931 - 38
1. Railroads, Local and light - Great Britain - History
2. Railroads, Local and light - Great Britain - History - Pictorial works
I. Title
385.5'0941'09043

ISBN 1 874498 03 2

Printed by
The Burlington Press
1 Station Road, Foxton, Cambridge CB2 6SW

Published by
Ross-Evans
St. Mary's House, 47 High Street, Trumpington,
Cambridge CB2 2HZ

PREFACE

In the 1930s I was a young railway enthusiast determined to visit and photograph all the small independent railways in existence in England and Wales. More than twenty of these small lines had not been included in the 'Big Four' railways formed at the Grouping in 1923. About half were standard gauge, the others were of various narrow gauges. Many were designated as 'Light Railways', with less strict laws about their operation.

This is the story of my 'adventures' as I explored these railways, illustrated by over seventy photographs taken on my travels. I hope this will be of interest to those who were not around to witness at first hand so many Light Railways that were still struggling to survive.

I wish to thank especially two people who gave me support and help throughout the composition of this book. Phil Atkins, Librarian of the National Railway Museum at York, helped me to extract much of my original data which I had deposited with the Museum. He also completed my Bradshaw timetable records. John K. Williams encouraged me to start on the project and could always be relied on to fill in gaps in my memory and to correct it when it was wrong. I am grateful to my daughter Ann for her work in designing the cover.

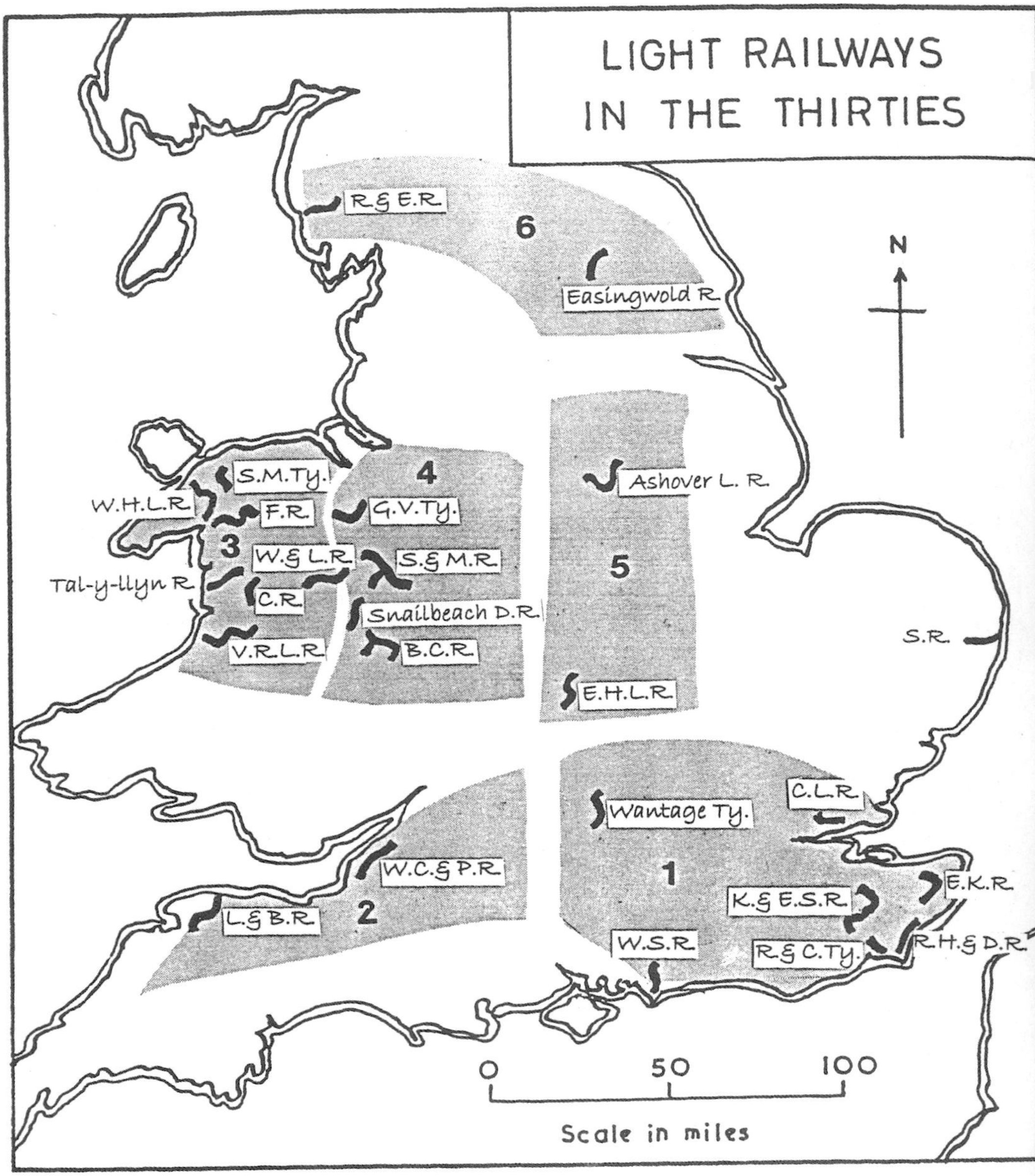

LIGHT RAILWAYS IN THE THIRTIES
R.& E.R.
6
Easingwold R.
N
4
S.M.Ty.
W.H.L.R.
F.R.
G.V.Ty.
Ashover L. R.
3
W.& L.R.
S.& M.R.
5
Tal-y-llyn R.
C.R.
Snailbeach D.R.
V.R.L.R.
B.C.R.
S.R.
E.H.L.R.
C.L.R.
Wantage Ty.
W.C.& P.R.
1
E.K.R.
K.& E.S.R.
L.& B.R.
2
W.S.R.
R.& C.Ty.
R.H.& D.R.
0
50
100
Scale in miles

CONTENTS

Introduction 1

Chapter 1 South East

Corringham Light Railway 4
East Kent Railway 6
Kent and East Sussex Railway 13
Romney Hythe and Dymchurch Railway 21
Hundred of Manhood and Selsey Tramways (West Sussex Railway) 24
Wantage Tramway 28
Rye and Camber Tramway 32

Chapter 2 South West

Lynton and Barnstaple Railway 36
Weston Clevedon and Portishead Light Railway 41

Chapter 3 Wales

Corris Railway 48
Tal-y-Llyn Railway 51
Festiniog Railway 55
Welsh Highland Railway 60
Snowdon Mountain Railway 65
Vale of Rheidol Light Railway 68
Welshpool and Llanfair Light Railway 70

Chapter 4 Welsh Borders

Bishop's Castle Railway 74
Glyn Valley Tramway 79
Shropshire and Montgomeryshire Railway 82
Snailbeach District Railways 87

Chapter 5 Central

Edge Hill Light Railway 92
Ashover Light Railway 95

Chapter 6 North

Easingwold Railway 100
Ravenglass and Eskdale Railway 102

Afterthoughts 105

INTRODUCTION

In 1931 there were no books about Light Railways that I had seen. Things had become very different by the end of the century, with books on every aspect of railways easily available at bookshops and railway stations. In these early days my only sources of information were occasional notes in the *Railway Magazine*, the *Locòmotive Magazine*, and the *Journal of the Stephenson Locomotive Society*. A valuable source was the wide selection of railway photographs which I used to consult at the Locomotive Publishing Company's premises at 3 Amen Corner, in London.

A priceless discovery was the *Railway Year Book* of 1931, published by the *Railway Magazine*. This contained a list of *'Remaining British Railways Owning Rolling Stock',* giving the name of each of these railways, its gauge and total length of track, the date when the line was opened and whether it had been authorised as a Light Railway. The number of locomotives was stated, and finally the name and address of the manager was given.

With the list of all the railways I wanted to visit, I prepared a map (next to the contents page) to show their distribution all over the country. The names of the towns and villages served by these railways could be found in Bradshaw's Guide, which gave the timetables of all the operating railways in Great Britain and Ireland. Lastly, by consulting Ordnance Survey maps, I drew larger scale maps to help me find the places I wished to visit.

For several years I planned my school and university holidays by train, cycling and walking to visit and photograph all these railways. In this book I describe the twenty-four railways visited, with the original maps and timetables, and the photographs I took on my travels.

For ease of access for the reader, the railways have been arranged into six geographical areas which have been superimposed on my original map. The spelling of names conforms to the conventions of the 1930s.

Chapter One

South East

CORRINGHAM LIGHT RAILWAY

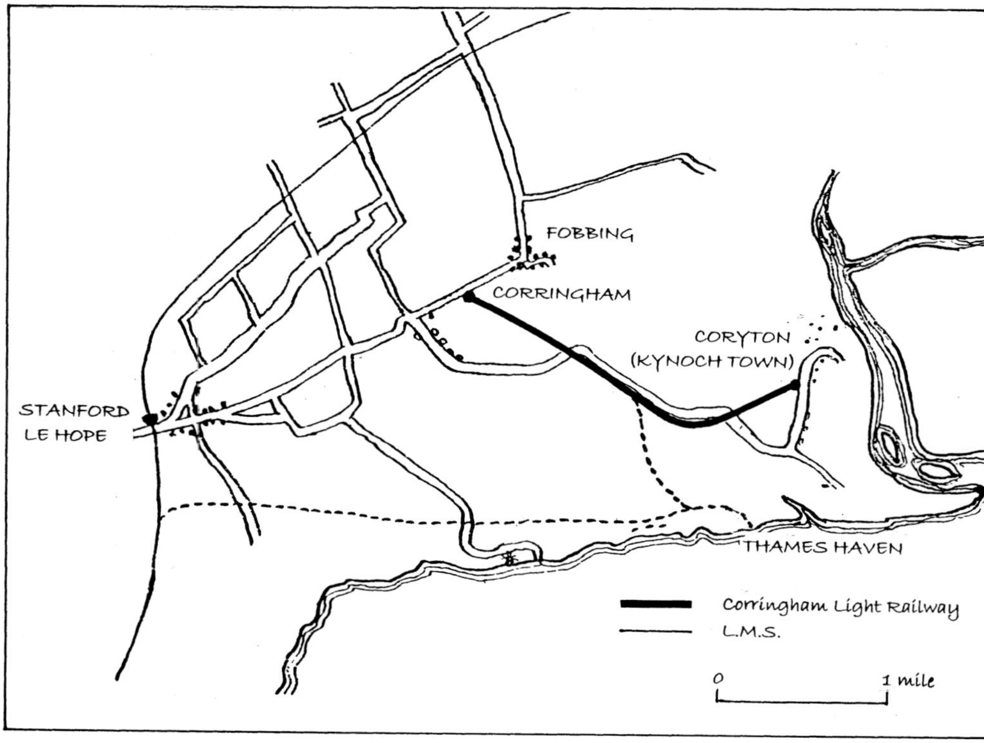

The Corringham Light Railway, a short standard gauge line just under three miles long, was opened in 1901 under a Light Railway Order.

It was built primarily to carry workers between Corringham and the works at Kynochtown where Kynoch Ltd had built a special village to house the hundreds of workers at their Explosive Works. Messrs Kynoch had been sold to Cory Bros. Ltd in 1921, and the name of Kynochtown was changed to Coryton. The rail journey took only seven minutes and at one time there was a service of seven trains a day in each direction. The timetable did not appear in *Bradshaw*, and at the time of my visit the service was much reduced.

I photographed one of the two engines that existed (figure 1.1). Both were Avonside 0-6-0ST, works numbers 1672 of 1914 and 1771 of 1917.

Figure 1.1 0-6-0ST, Avonside no.1771 of 1917.

At Corringham Station things were very quiet and nobody seemed to be about. It became apparent that stray passengers were not encouraged, for as I stood on the deserted platform an official approached, and to my surprise asked me, 'Do you know you are trespassing?' This made it clear to me that, although it was actually a public railway, the Corringham Light Railway was almost entirely used by the workers of the factory at the other end of the line.

During the Second World War the railway was not taken over by the Railway Executive but officially stopped carrying passengers. In 1948 it escaped Nationalisation, and in 1952 the last train ran and the track was lifted.

EAST KENT RAILWAY

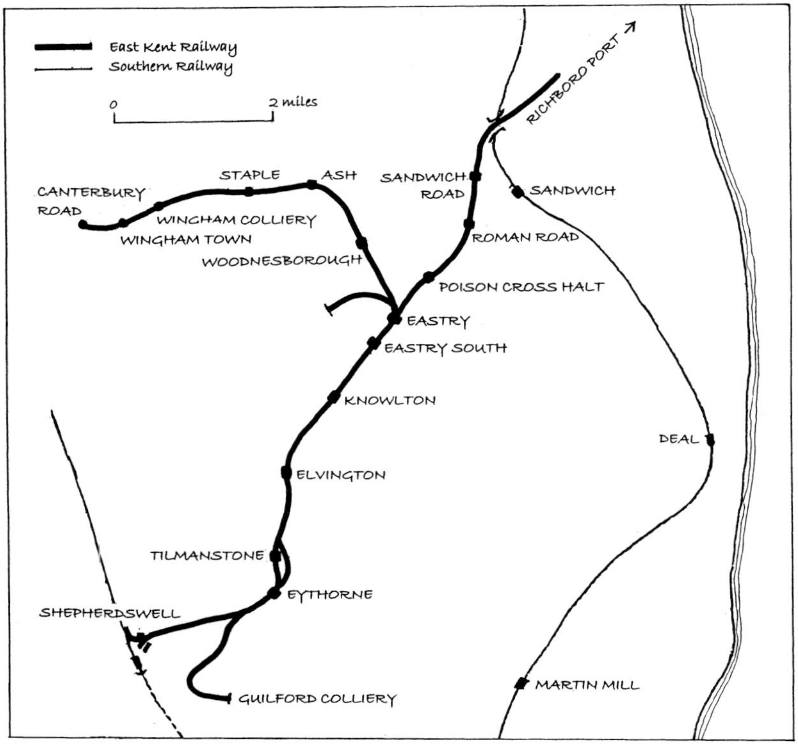

SHEPHERD'S WELL, SANDWICH ROAD, and CANTERBURY ROAD.—East Kent.

Miles from Shepherd's Well	Down.	Week Days only. mrn	aft E	aft S
	348 London (Victoria) ...dep.	9 4	2 5	2 12
	348 " (Charing Cross) "	8 18	..	..
	348 " (Cannon St.) "	..	..	..
	348 " (London B'dge) "	8 26	..	..
	Shepherd's Well ....dep.	12 5	4 45	5 20
1¾	Eythorne	1212	4 52	5 27
2½	Elvington	1215	4 55	5 30
3¼	Knowlton	1219	4 59	5 34
5¼	Eastry, South	Aa	Aa	Aa
5¾	Eastry B	1227	5 7	5 41
6¼	Poison Cross Halt	..	..	..
7¼	Roman Road C	..	..	..
8	Sandwich Road ....arr.	..	..	..
6¾	Woodnesborough	1231	5 11	5 45
8	Ash Town	1235	5 15	5 50
8¾	Staple	1238	5 18	5 54
10¼	Wingham Colliery	1243	5 23	6 0
10¾	Wingham Town	1245	5 25	6 3
11¼	Canterbury Road D ....arr.	1247	5 27	6 5

Aa Stops when required. B Station for Sandwich. C Roman Road, Woodnesborough.
D Canterbury Road, Wingham. E or E Except Sats. S or S Sats. only.

This 11¼ mile long standard gauge line was opened in 1911 to serve the East Kent coalfields. It was also hoped that the railway would play a part in developing the port of Richborough.

I visited the East Kent Railway several times but never travelled much on the line as the passenger service was very limited. However I managed to photograph all eight locomotives as I saw them around the works and sheds at Shepherdswell.

The invaluable 1931 Railway Year Book gave the name of Colonel H.F. Stephens of Tonbridge, Kent as the railway manager. He was also quoted as being the manager of no less than eight other independent railways, all of which I managed to explore in due time. Colonel Stephens has become an almost legendary name in recent years, but he died in 1931 and I was never privileged to meet him. All his railways seemed to be on the edge of financial disaster, but were kept alive by the devotion of men who kept faith in them.

The first two photographs of the East Kent Railway show different saddle tank engines. Figure 1.2 shows 0-6-0ST, No.2 *Walton Park* departing from Shepherdswell, bound for Eastry, with a mixed train consisting of one coach and about six wagons. This engine, built by Hudswell Clarke, no.823 of 1908, had a complicated history. She was transferred by Colonel Stephens from the Shropshire and Montgomeryshire Railway, having been originally supplied to the Weston Clevedon and Portishead Railway.

Figure 1.2 0-6-0ST, *Walton Park*, Hudswell Clarke no.823 of 1908, leaving Shepherdswell.

Figure 1.3 shows E.K.R. *No.1*, another 0-6-0ST built by Fox Walker no.271 of 1875. This was formerly Great Western Railway No.1386 and was bought by Colonel Stephens in 1911.

Figure 1.3 0-6-0ST, No.1, ex G.W.R. No.1386, Fox Walker no.271 of 1875.

I took the photograph of East Kent Railway *No.4* (figure 1.4), a quite massive 0-6-0T, just after a major overhaul, and the connecting rod not yet refitted. She looked very impressive painted in Southern Railway green livery! She was built by Kerr Stuart, no.3067 in 1917 and came here from the War Department.

The next three engines I photographed were of special interest to me as they were formerly owned by the London and South Western Railway where I spent most of my young days.

East Kent Railway *No 3* (figure 1.5) was in a dilapidated state, but could still be recognised from a drawing I had recently seen in the Locomotive Magazine. This showed it to be an un-rebuilt example of an 'Ilfracombe Goods' engine, with the big dome above the firebox sand and the ornamental splashers over the driving wheels. She was built by Beyer Peacock in 1880, and although bought by the

East Kent Railway in 1918, the old L.S.W.R. number 394 was still visible on the side of the cab in 1932.

Figure 1.4 0-6-0T, No.4, ex I.W.D., Kerr Stuart no.3067 of 1917, repainted after overhaul.

Figure 1.5 0-6-0, No.3, ex L.S.W.R. No.394, Ilfracombe Goods, Beyer Peacock, 1880.

No.5, a 4-4-2T, built by Neilson, no.3209 of 1885 (figure 1.6), was another ex L.S.W.R. locomotive and held a very special memory for me. My grandparents had retired to Devon, not far from Axminster, and every year I made the train journey to see them. I had previously met two similar Adams 4-4-2 tank engines working on the Lyme Regis branch line. At one time there had been over a hundred of these handsome engines operating suburban services around London, but after electrification they all disappeared.

This one survived because the L.S.W.R. had sold her in 1917 to the Ministry of Munitions for £2,104 to work at the Ridham Salvage Depot near Sittingbourne. In 1919 she was resold for £900 to the East Kent Railway where I saw her in 1933.

Figure 1.6 4-4-2T, No.5, ex L.S.W.R. No.488, Neilson no.3209 of 1885. Sold in 1946 to the Southern Railway and later to the Bluebell Railway.

The third engine of special interest was the 0-6-0ST No.7 also from the L.S.W.R. where she had been No.0127 (figure 1.7). This was one of a standard design by Beyer Peacock, some of which I had previously seen and photographed at Eastleigh. I had some difficulty in photographing No.7, because, during my earlier visits, she always seemed to be in the shed. However on my third visit, one year later,

I was delighted to find that the building had fallen down, and so I was able to take the picture shown.

Figure 1.7 0-6-0ST, No.7, ex L.S.W.R. No.0127, Beyer Peacock,1882.

Figure 1.8 0-6-0, No.6, ex S.E.C.R. No.372 of 1891.

Both No.6 and No.8 were ex Chatham Railway 0-6-0 goods engines and were responsible for much of the heavier work on the railway. No.6 had formerly been no.372 and was built in 1891. No.8 had been no.376 and was built in the same year. Figures 1.8 and 1.9 show the different appearances of these two engines. No.6 had been fitted with an O1 boiler in 1932, whereas No.8 retained a domeless boiler and cut-down chimney from her previous use on the Canterbury and Whitstable Railway.

Figure 1.9 0-6-0, No.8, ex S.E.C.R. No.376 of 1891, showing the cut down chimney and dome from working on the Canterbury and Whitstable Railway.

After the Second World War the railway closed down in sections, and by 1995 only a two mile section from Shepherdswell to the colliery remained.

It is notable that the Adams 4-4-2T No.5 did not end her career on the East Kent Railway. In 1946 the Southern had both the Lyme Regis Adams tank engines under repair and purchased E.K.R. No.5. After being overhauled she was put to work and survived to become British Rail No.30583. The three engines were withdrawn in 1961 and No.488 went to the Bluebell Railway where her true value has been much appreciated.

KENT AND EAST SUSSEX RAILWAY

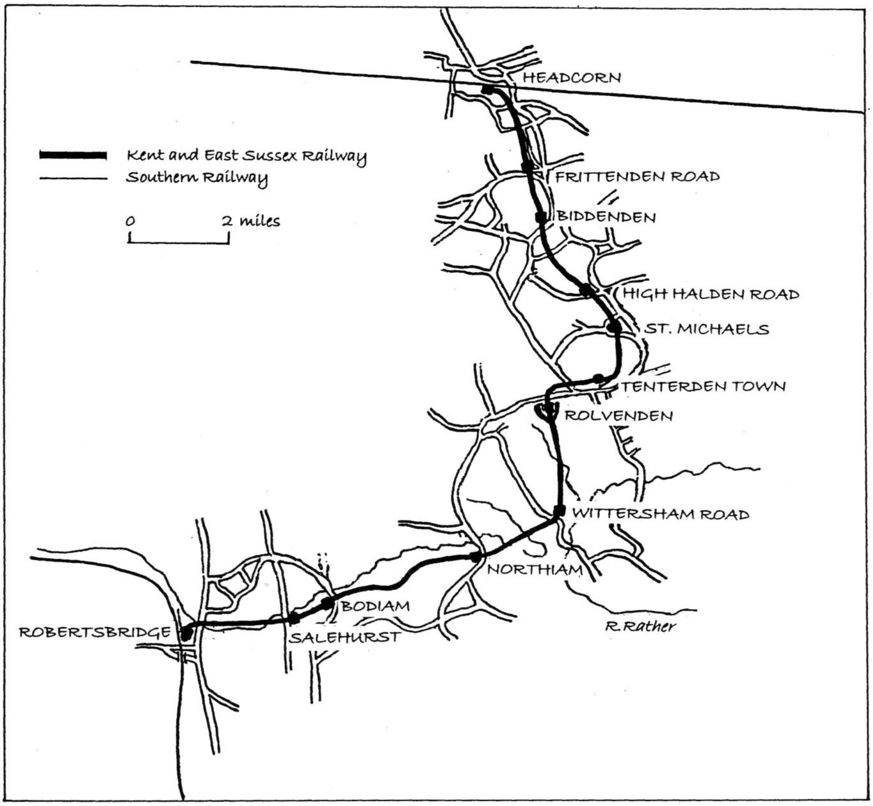

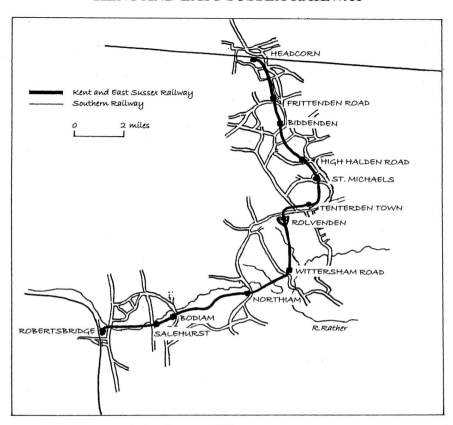

Robertsbridge and Headcorn.] 1086

ROBERTSBRIDGE, TENTERDEN TOWN, and HEADCORN.—Kent and East Sussex.

Miles from Robertsbridge.	Down.	Week Days only. mrn	mrn	mrn	aft (Saturdays only.)	aft (Except Saturdays.)	aft (Except Saturdays.)	aft (Saturdays only.)
	Charing Cross Station, 340 London .... dep.			9 15			4 18	5 20
	340 " (Cannon St.) "			9 12				
	340 " (Lndn B'dge) "		5 30	9 17			4 25	
	343 Hastings .... "		7 45	1025			5 16	5 16
	Robertsbridge .... dep.		8 15	1115			6 5	6 45
1¼	Salehurst Platform		Bb	Bb			Bb	Bb
2½	Junction Road		Aa	Aa			Aa	Aa
3½	Bodiam, for Staplecross		8 25	1130			6 14	6 55
7	Northiam **A**		8 35	1145			6 23	7 4
9½	Wittersham Road		8 42	12 0			6 30	7 11
12	Rolvenden		8 49	1210			6 36	7 18
13½	**Tenterden Town**	8 0	8 54	1215	3 40	3 40	6 40	7 23
14½	Tenterden St. Michaels	Aa			Aa	Aa		
15¾	High Halden Road	8 10			3 50	3 50		
13	Biddenden	8 20			4 0	4 0		
19½	Frittenden Road	Aa			Aa	Aa		
21½	**Headcorn 322, 330** ..... arr.	8 35			4 20	4 20		
67½	**330 London** (Lndn B'dge) arr.	10 3			6 6			
68	330 " (Cannon St.) "	10 8			6 12			
69½	330 " (Charing X.) "					6 22		

A Station for Beckley and Sandhurst. **Aa** Stop when required.
Bb Stops when required by signal during daylight only.

The Kent and East Sussex Railway started life as the Rother Valley Railway running from Robertsbridge, on the Tonbridge-Eastbourne line, to Tenterden in Kent. It was opened in 1900 under the management of Colonel Stephens and was extended a further eight miles to Headcorn in 1905, when it was renamed the Kent and East Sussex Railway.

This was one of the first light railways I visited and the whole day in April 1932 was one of my most delightful experiences. It started when I arrived at Robertsbridge Station and found No.2, one of the ex Rother Valley 2-4-0T engines, standing in the bay with a train consisting of one passenger carriage and several wagons. The locomotive was painted dark blue with K.& E.S.R. lettering encircling the name *Northiam* in the centre (figure 1.10).

Figure 1.10 Former Rother Valley Railway 2-4-0T, No.2 *Northiam*, Hawthorn Leslie no.2421 of 1899.

We set off on the thirteen mile journey to Tenterden which acccording to the timetable was booked to take one hour. It was soon clear that it was going to take much longer than this for, at each station, the train was split up for some extensive shunting, and for social chit-chat. After a pleasant hour-and-a-half I, being the only passenger, was safely delivered to the shed and works at Rolvenden.

On arrival at the shed I could see several interesting locomotives. Some of these were in and around the shed. However no less than three of them were standing in a dismantled state in a siding behind the buildings.

On a visit over a year later, one of the engines in steam was No.4, a freshly painted green ex L.S.W.R. 0-6-0ST No.0335, built by Beyer Peacock, no.1596 of 1876 (figure 1.11). She had recently arrived, together with two spare boilers, from the Southern Railway in exchange for the big 0-8-0T, *Hecate*.

Figure 1.11 0-6-0ST, No.4, ex L.S.W.R. No.0335.

Figure 1.12 2-4-0T, No.1 *Tenterden*, built by Hawthorn Leslie in 1899.

Other active engines I photographed in 1932 at Rolvenden included No.1 *Tenterden* (figure 1.12), which was the other original one from the Rother Valley Railway. *Tenterden* and *Northiam* were both built by Hawthorn Leslie in 1899, works numbers 2420 and 2421.

The next locomotive was 0-6-0 No.9, *Juno,* an ex L.S.W.R. Ilfracombe Goods engine, built by Beyer Peacock in 1873, no.1210, later rebuilt by Adams (figure 1.13). The front view of *Juno* (figure 1.14) shows that the smoke-box door is hinged on the "wrong" side. The reason given to me was that the doors were sometimes burned through as a result of fires forming at the bottom of the smoke-box. This was overcome by fixing a patch on the door and hinging it on the other side!

Figure 1.13 0-6-0, No.9 *Juno*, ex L.S.W.R. built by Beyer Peacock in 1873.

The three woebegone examples on the siding behind the shed turned out to be No.7 *Rother*, another ex L.S.W.R. 0-6-0, (figure 1.15) and two ex Brighton Terriers, No.3 *Bodiam* (figure 1.16) and No.5 *Rolvenden.*

One engine I did not photograph was No.8 *Hesperus*, 0-6-0ST by Manning Wardle, no.630 of 1876. This had come to the K.E.S.R. via the Great Western Railway and acquired some Swindon characteristics on the way.

Figure 1.14 Front view of No.9 *Juno*.

Figure 1.15 No.7 *Rother*.

Figure 1.16 No.3 *Bodiam*.

In the following year I visited the K.E.S.R. again and photographed No.2 *Northiam* about to take her train out of Tenterden (figure 1.17).

A few years later I was to see this engine again when she appeared in the Will Hay film '*Oh Mr. Porter'* under the name of *Gladstone*. Unfortunately the film company had fitted a rather silly tall spiked chimney; but in spite of this I do remember enjoying the film. There were many shots of *Gladstone* and I was glad that Will Hay and his team treated the venerable locomotive with appropriate love and respect. I believe that No.2 returned to Rolvenden in 1937 and was withdrawn soon afterwards.

Figure 1.17 2-4-0T, No.2 *Northiam* at Tenterden station.

Another photograph I took about this time was of 0-8-0T, *Hecate.* former No.4 of the K.E.S.R. This engine had been exchanged for the 0-6-0ST, the new No.4 shown in figure 1.11. I came across her at the Nine Elms sheds on the Southern Railway (figure 1.18).

Figure 1.18 Former K.E.S.R. 0-8-0T *Hecate* seen on the Southern Railway.

Figure 1.19 A Ford railcar set.

During World War II, the K.E.S.R. track was taken over by the military, but in 1945 the railway reverted for a short time to W.H.Austen, the successor to Colonel Stephens. Some improvements were then made, including the overhaul of Terrier No.3, which appeared at Rolvenden resplendent in Malachite green! However, in spite of this, the line was closed by British Rail in 1961.

As the result of the efforts of a preservation society, some of the railway began to operate again in 1974.

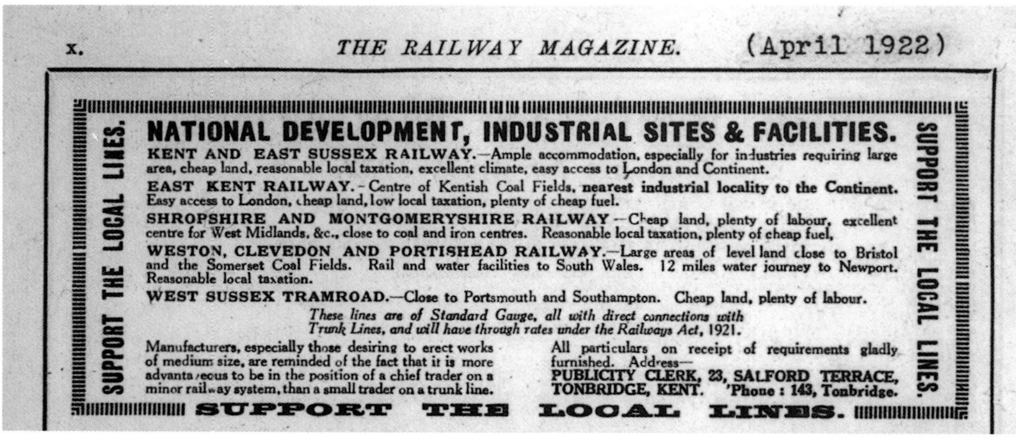

x. *THE RAILWAY MAGAZINE.* (April 1922)

SUPPORT THE LOCAL LINES.

NATIONAL DEVELOPMENT, INDUSTRIAL SITES & FACILITIES.

KENT AND EAST SUSSEX RAILWAY.—Ample accommodation, especially for industries requiring large area, cheap land, reasonable local taxation, excellent climate, easy access to London and Continent.

EAST KENT RAILWAY.—Centre of Kentish Coal Fields, **nearest industrial locality to the Continent.** Easy access to London, cheap land, low local taxation, plenty of cheap fuel.

SHROPSHIRE AND MONTGOMERYSHIRE RAILWAY—Cheap land, plenty of labour, excellent centre for West Midlands, &c., close to coal and iron centres. Reasonable local taxation, plenty of cheap fuel.

WESTON, CLEVEDON AND PORTISHEAD RAILWAY.—Large areas of level land close to Bristol and the Somerset Coal Fields. Rail and water facilities to South Wales. 12 miles water journey to Newport. Reasonable local taxation.

WEST SUSSEX TRAMROAD.—Close to Portsmouth and Southampton. Cheap land, plenty of labour.

These lines are of Standard Gauge, all with direct connections with Trunk Lines, and will have through rates under the Railways Act, 1921.

Manufacturers, especially those desiring to erect works of medium size, are reminded of the fact that it is more advantageous to be in the position of a chief trader on a minor railway system, than a small trader on a trunk line.

All particulars on receipt of requirements gladly furnished. Address—
PUBLICITY CLERK, 23, SALFORD TERRACE, TONBRIDGE, KENT. 'Phone : 143, Tonbridge.

SUPPORT THE LOCAL LINES.

SUPPORT THE LOCAL LINES.

An advertisement of local lines from the April 1922 Railway Magazine in the office of Colonel Stephens at Tonbridge.

ROMNEY HYTHE AND DYMCHURCH RAILWAY

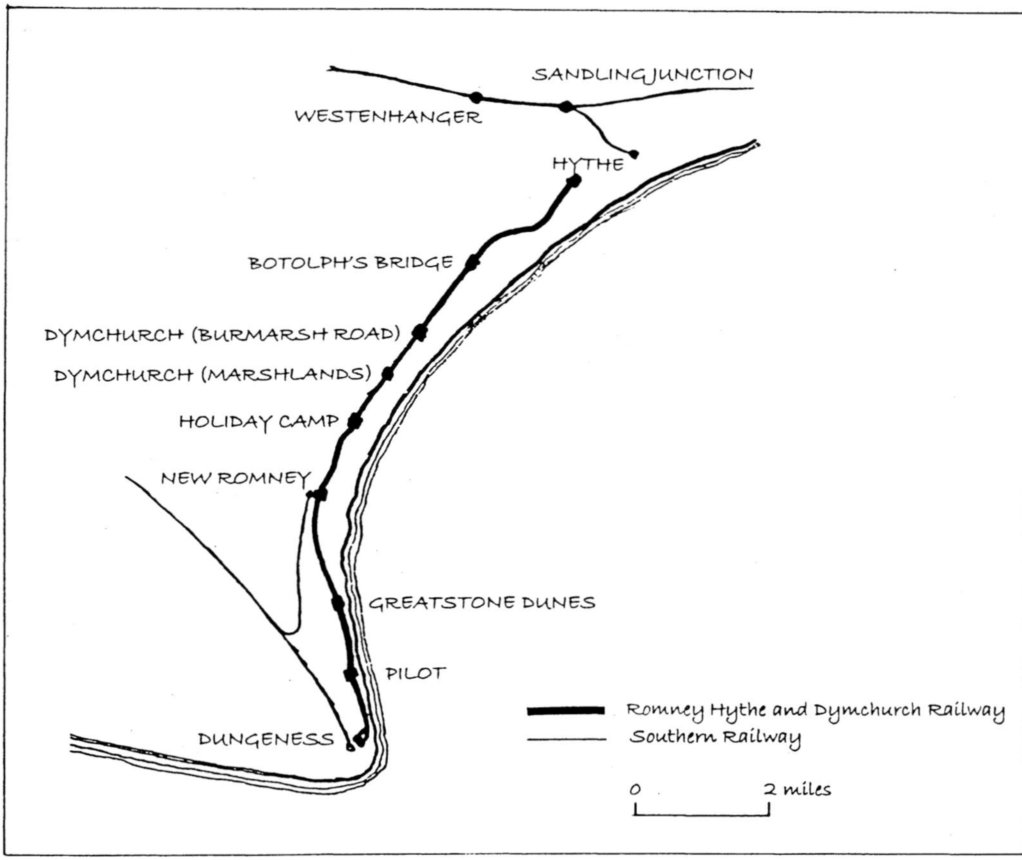

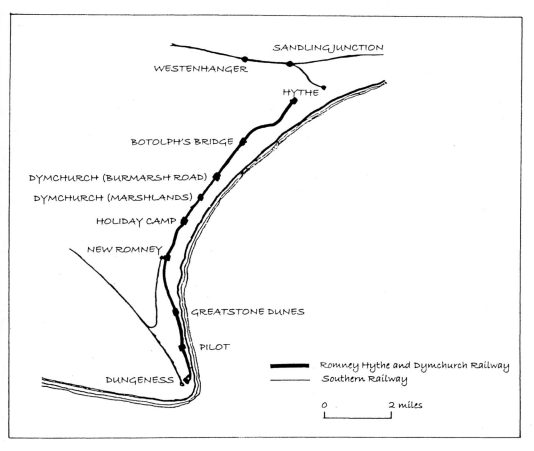

DUNGENESS, NEW ROMNEY, DYMCHURCH, and HYTHE.—Romney, Hythe, and Dymchurch.

Week Days and Sundays.

Miles		mrn	mrn	mrn	mrn	mrn	mrn	non	aft	aft	aft	aft	aft	aft	aft	aft	aft	aft	aft	aft	aft	aft	
	Dungeness (Light House) ..dep.	....	....	**A**	..	**A**	....	12 0	**A**	..	**A**	....	**A**	....	....	**A**	4 15	**A**	....	**A**	6 0	7 30	....
1	The Pilot	..	..	..	....	..	..	12 5	..	....	..	..	..	..	..	..	4 20	..	..	..	6 5	7 35	..
—	Maddieson's Camp	....	9 45	....	11 0	....	1145	1210	....	1245	....	1 45	....	2 45	3 15	....	4 25	....	....	....	6 10	7 40	....
4	Greatstone	..	9 50	..	11 5	..	1150	1215	..	1250	..	1 50	..	2 50	3 20	..	4 30	..	..	..	6 15	7 45	..
5	**New Romney**	9 30	10 0	1030	1115	....	12 0	1230	....	1 0	....	2 0	....	3 0	3 30	....	4 45	....	5 30	....	6 30	8 0	....
7	Holiday Camp	9 38	10 8	1038	1123	..	12 8	1238	..	1 8	..	2 8	..	3 8	3 38	..	4 53	..	5 38	..	6 38	8 8	..
8¾	**Dymchurch**	9 45	1015	1045	1130	1150	1215	1245	1 0	1 15	1 50	2 15	2 50	3 15	3 45	4 15	5 0	5 15	5 45	6 0	6 45	8 15	....
9¾	Burmarsh Road	9 50	1020	1050	1135	1155	1220	1250	1 5	1 20	1 55	2 20	2 55	3 20	3 50	4 20	5 5	5 20	5 50	6 5	6 50	8 20	..
13¾	**Hythe** (Kent) **322, 330** ....arr.	10 0	1030	11 0	1145	12 5	1230	1 0	1 15	1 30	2 5	2 30	3 5	3 30	4 0	4 30	5 15	5 30	6 0	6 15	7 0	8 30	....

Mls		mrn	mrn	mrn	non	aft	aft	aft	aft	aft	aft	aft	aft	aft	aft	aft	aft	aft	aft	aft	aft	aft	
	Hythe (Kent) ....dep.	1030	11 0	1130	12 0	1230	1 0	1 30	2 0	2 30	2 45	3 15	3 40	4 0	4 30	5 0	5 35	6 0	6 30	7 0	7 45	9 0	..
4	**Burmarsh Road**	1040	1110	1140	1210	1240	1 10	1 40	2 10	2 40	2 55	3 25	3 50	4 10	4 40	5 10	5 45	6 10	6 40	7 10	7 55	9 10	....
5	**Dymchurch**	1045	1115	1145	1215	1245	1 15	1 45	2 15	2 45	3 0	3 30	3 55	4 15	4 45	5 15	5 50	6 15	6 45	7 15	8 0	9 15	..
6¾	**Holiday Camp**	1052	1122	**A**	1222	**A**	1 22	**A**	2 22	**A**	3 7	3 37	**A**	4 22	4 52	**A**	**A**	6 22	6 52	7 22	8 7	9 22	....
8¾	**New Romney 347**	11 0	1130	..	1230	..	1 30	..	2 30	..	3 15	3 45	..	4 30	5 0	..	..	6 30	7 0	7 30	8 15	9 30	..
9¾	**Greatstone**	11 6	1136	....	1236	....	1 36	....	2 36	....	3 21	....	....	....	5 6	....	....	6 36	7 6	**A**	....	....	....
—	Maddieson's Camp	1111	1141	..	1241	..	1 41	..	2 41	..	3 26	..	..	..	5 11	..	..	6 41	7 11	..	..	..	..
12¾	The Pilot ....[347	1118	....	....	....	....	....	....	....	....	3 33	....	....	....	5 18	....	....	6 48	....	....	....	....	....
13¾	**Dungeness** (Light House) arr.	1130	..	..	..	..	..	..	..	..	3 45	4 0	..	..	5 30	..	..	7 0	..	..	..	..	..

A Weather permitting.

Running between Hythe and Dymchurch on the south coast of Kent this fourteen mile long railway was opened in 1927 by Captain Howey as a fully equipped railway on the 15 inch gauge to carry passengers and goods. It has been described as a one-third size scale model of a main line railway.

My parents used to take me as a child for summer holidays at Hythe, so although I much admired the scale model Gresley Pacifics, there remained no exciting discoveries for me to make on this highly efficient and rather remarkable railway.

Below is a list of the their locomotives together with photographs of two of the handsome Pacifics (figures 1.20 and 1.21).

No.1	4-6-2	*Green Goddess*
No.2	4-6-2	*Northern Chief*
No.3	4-6-2	*Southern Maid*
No.4	0-4-0	*The Bug*
No.5	4-8-2	*Hercules*
No.6	4-8-2	*Samson*
No.7	4-6-2	*Typhoon*
No.8	4-6-2	*Hurricane*
No.9	4-6-2	*Black Prince*
No.10	4-6-2	*Dr. Syn*

Figure 1 20 4-6-2 *Green Goddess.*

Figure 1.21 4-6-2 *Dr. Syn.*

HUNDRED OF MANHOOD AND SELSEY TRAMWAYS
Later became WEST SUSSEX RAILWAY

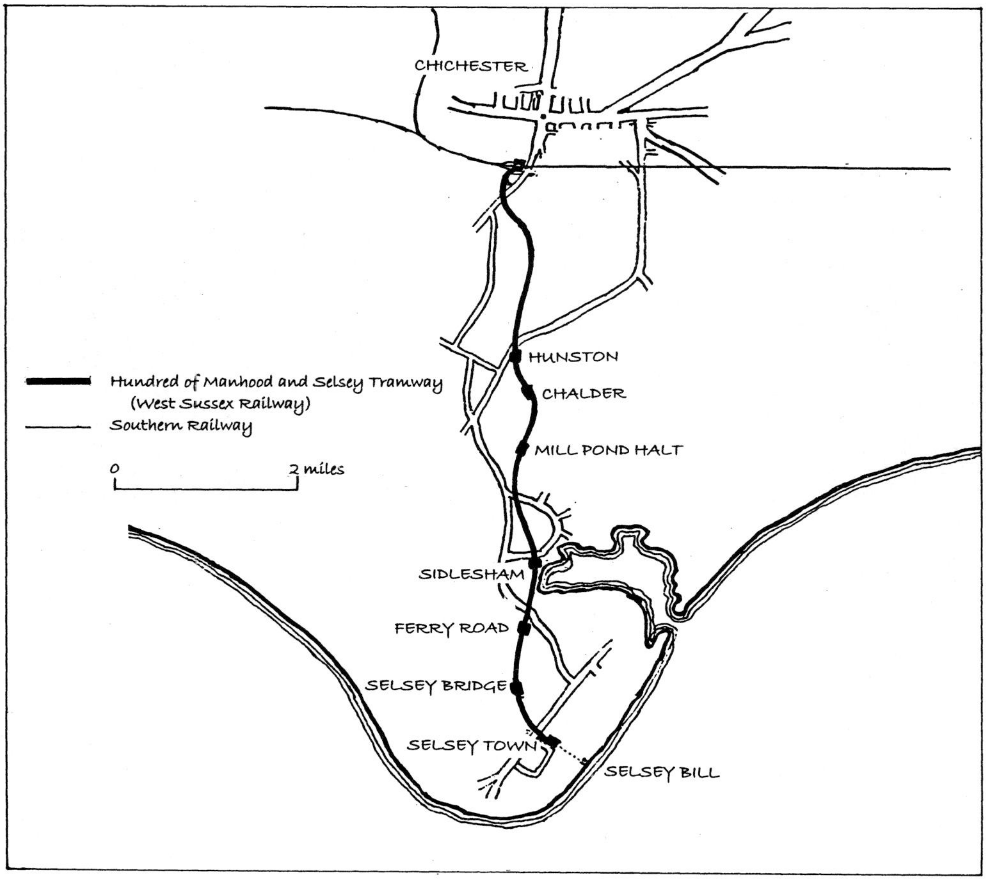

SELSEY TOWN and CHICHESTER (**Motor Cars—3rd class only**).—West Sussex.

Miles	**Up.**	Week Days only.										
		mrn		mrn		aft		aft		aft		Saturdays only. aft
	Selsey Town............dep.	8 10	..	10 0	..	1 10	..	3 10	..	5 30	..	7 15
¼	Selsey Bridge................	8 11	..	10 2	..	1 11	..	3 11	..	5 31	..	7 16
2¼	Ferry..........................	8 16	..	10 8	..	1 16	..	3 16	..	5 36	..	7 21
2¾	Sidlesham....................	8 21	..	1013	..	1 21	..	3 21	..	5 41	..	7 26
3¼	Mill Pond Halt..............	8 23	..	1015	..	1 23	..	3 23	..	5 43	..	7 28
4	Chalder.......................	8 26	..	1018	..	1 26	..	3 26	..	5 46	..	7 31
5½	Hunston...............[268	8 31	..	1027	..	1 31	..	3 31	..	5 51	..	7 36
7¾	**Chichester 250, 258.** arr.	8 40	..	1040	..	1 40	..	3 40	..	6 0	..	7 45

Miles	**Down.**	Week Days only.										
		mrn	mrn		aft		aft		aft		Saturdays only. aft	
	Chichester..............dep.	9 15	1130	..	2 10	..	4 10	..	6 15	..	8 30	..
2¼	Hunston........................	9 24	1140	..	2 19	..	4 19	..	6 24	..	8 39	..
3¾	Chalder........................	9 29	1146	..	2 24	..	4 24	..	6 29	..	8 44	..
4½	Mill Pond Halt..............	9 32	1149	..	2 27	..	4 27	..	6 32	..	8 47	..
5	Sidlesham....................	9 34	1155	..	2 29	..	4 29	..	6 34	..	8 49	..
5½	Ferry..........................	9 39	12 1	..	2 34	..	4 34	..	6 39	..	8 54	..
7¼	Selsey Bridge................	9 44	1210	..	2 39	..	4 39	..	6 44	..	8 59	..
7¾	**Selsey Town**............arr.	9 45	1212	..	2 40	..	4 40	..	6 45	..	9 0	..

This standard gauge railway ran for almost eight miles from Chichester to Selsey on the South Coast. Opened in 1897 it was managed by Colonel Stephens and served the Manhood peninsula, usually known as Selsey Bill. It was named a 'tramway' because it was built and operated under the simpler rules than those applying to light railways. In 1924 the railway took a step towards becoming legal when it was established as the West Sussex Railway.

The railway was much loved by local people and performed a valuable service until the arrival of the motor-car in the 1920s. The first locomotive, 2-4-2T, No.1 *Selsey* was bought new from Peckett. This was the only new engine owned by the tramway. Colonel Stephens later acquired a series of second-hand locomotives, mostly Manning Wardle saddle tank engines, some of which gave good service.

The railway was nearing its end when I made my last visit and took the photographs shown. On this day the passengers were carried in one of Colonel Stephens' Shefflex railbus sets (figure 1.22). It was not a pleasant ride, in fact the noisiest and most uncomfortable rail journey I can remember. The best parts were when we had to stop in silence and drive sheep off the line!

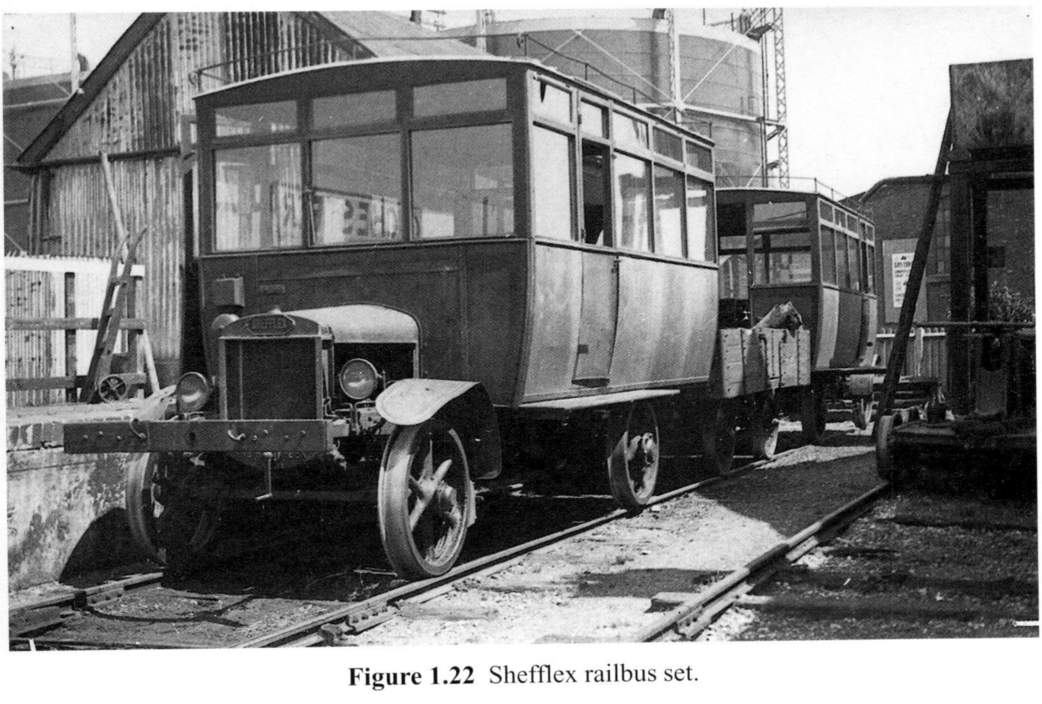

Figure 1.22 Shefflex railbus set.

There was one steam engine *Ringing Rock*, Manning Wardle no.890 of 1893, standing in the yard at Chichester (figure 1.23).

Figure 1.23 *Ringing Rock*, Manning Wardle no.890 of 1893.

I also saw a variety of passenger coaches and photographed some of these. The first was a smart six-wheeled coach with five compartments of third class built for the London, Chatham & Dover Railway in 1886 (figure 1.24). It continued its career on the Southern Railway until sold to the West Sussex Railway in 1931.

The other coach was altogether different (figure 1.25). A saloon coach with end-balconies, it is said to have been built for a South American railway, but came new in 1898 to the Lambourn Valley Railway as first and third composite No.2. Later it was sold by auction and came to Selsey in 1904.

The railway ran the last train on 19th January 1935.

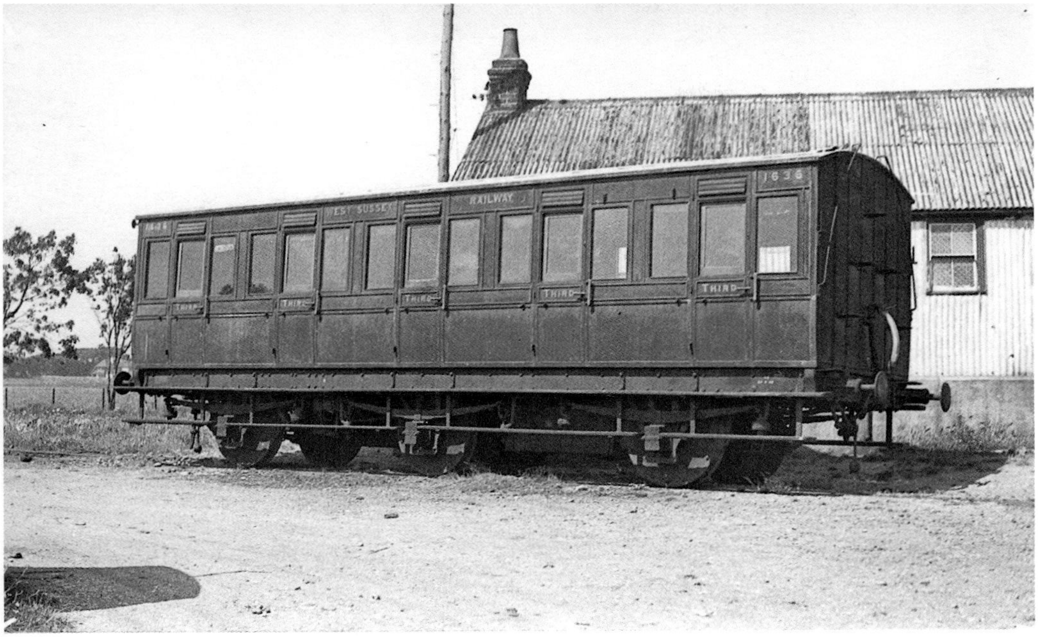

Figure 1.24 6-wheeled passenger coach.

Figure 1.25 Saloon coach with end-balconies.

WANTAGE TRAMWAY

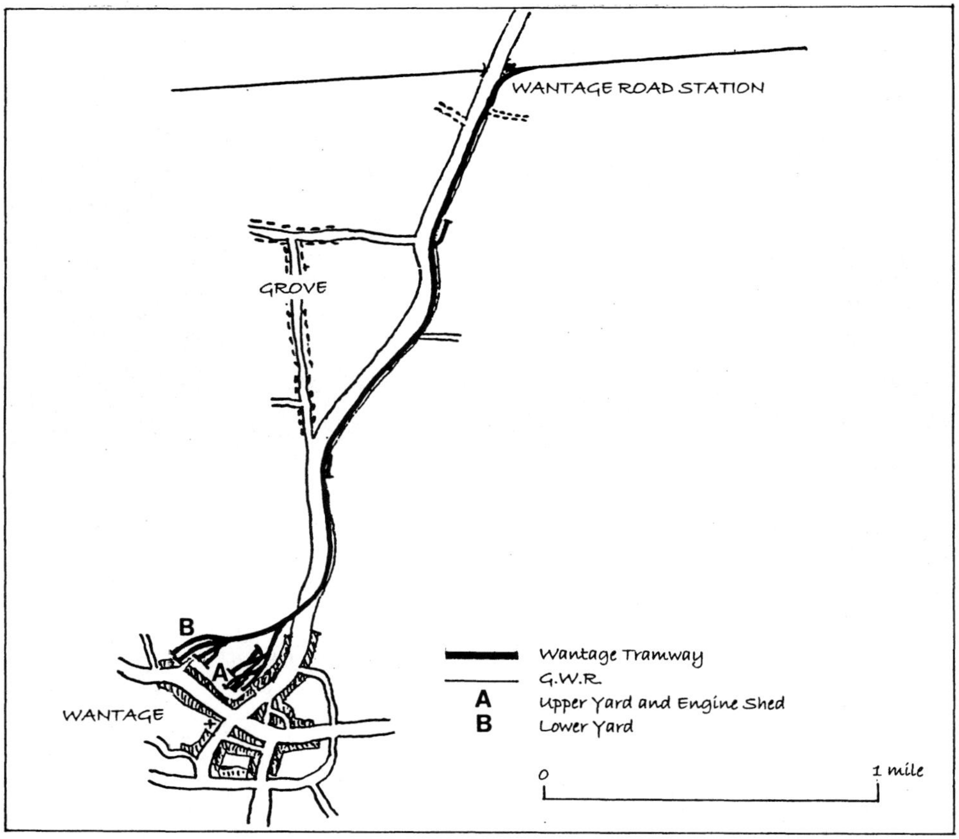

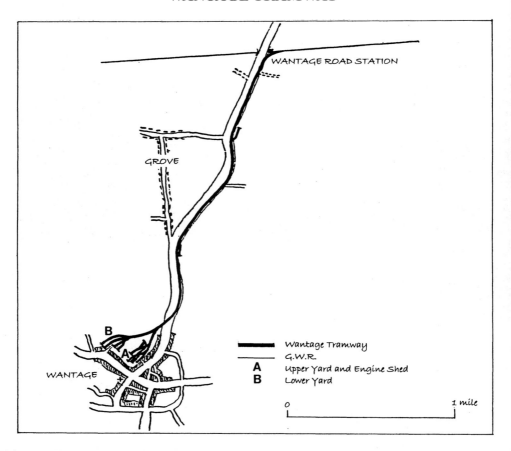

This standard gauge tramway ran for $2^1/_2$ miles alongside public roads from the town of Wantage in Berkshire to the Great Western railway station at Wantage Road. It opened in 1875 with horses as the motive power. After a short time steam trams started to operate and a fine series of tram engines and trailers appeared on this line.

I had seen some photographs of these tram-engines and trailers at the offices of the Locomotive Publishing Co. at 3 Amen Corner, but in 1935 when I first visited Wantage, these had all gone.

Although passenger services had ceased in July 1925, two interesting locomotives still operated. The older one was 0-4-0WT No.5 *Shannon,* built by George England in 1857 usually known as *Jane* (figure 1.26).

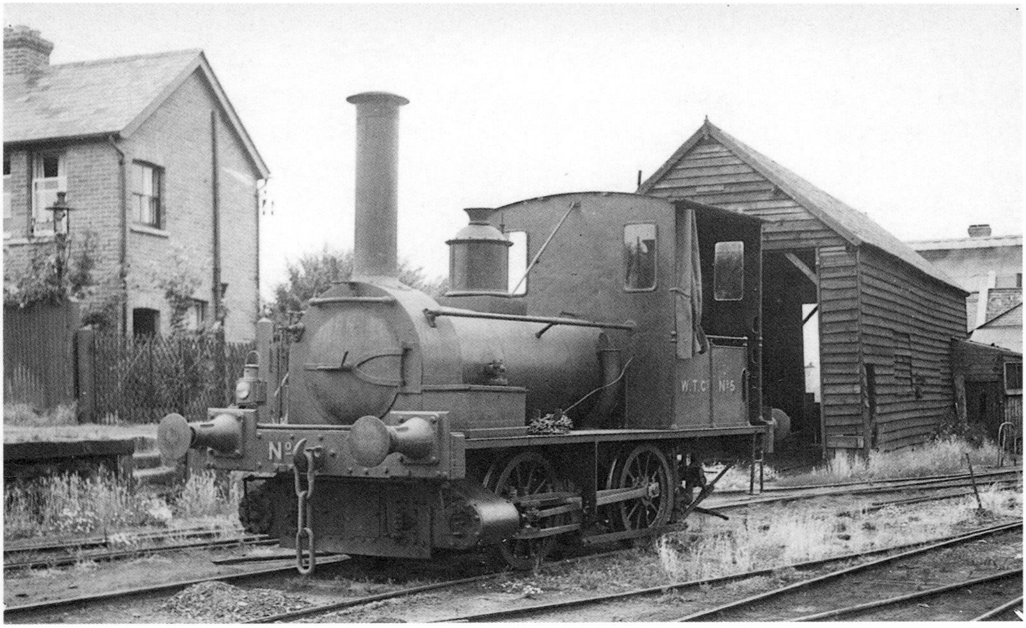

Figure 1.26 0-4-0WT, No.5 *Shannon* at Wantage Upper Yard.

Figure 1.27 0-4-0ST, No.7, sometimes known as *Mary*.

The other engine was 0-4-0ST No.7, Manning Wardle no.1057 of 1888 (figure 1.27). She had no official name but was known to the engine men as *Mary*. Before she joined the tramway in 1893 she had worked on the construction of the Manchester Ship Canal under the name of *Massey*. She operated until the tramway was closed in 1946. Among the others working on this site was the 0-4-0ST *Sankey* which I had seen on the ill-fated Edge Hill Light Railway.

Figure 1.28 Road alongside the Wantage Tramway.

Figure 1.29 Local history seen at Wantage.

The track ran alongside the Wantage Road as seen in figure 1.28. The tramway was subject to local jokes such as the story of one of the trams being sent to Swindon to be reversed on a turntable there and hence make the position of the steps more convenient. Another story with a ring of truth concerns Mr. Hitchcock and his donkey-cart. It is immortalised on the postcard which I bought at Wantage (figure 1.29).

The tramway was closed in 1946, and the plant and equipment sold by tender. *Shannon* was purchased by the Great Western Railway for £100 and was displayed on the station platform at Wantage Road where many years later I took her photograph (figure 1.30). When the station was closed in 1965 she was taken to Didcot and restored to working order.

Figure 1.30 I took my son to see *Shannon* at Wantage Road around 1960.

RYE AND CAMBER TRAMWAY

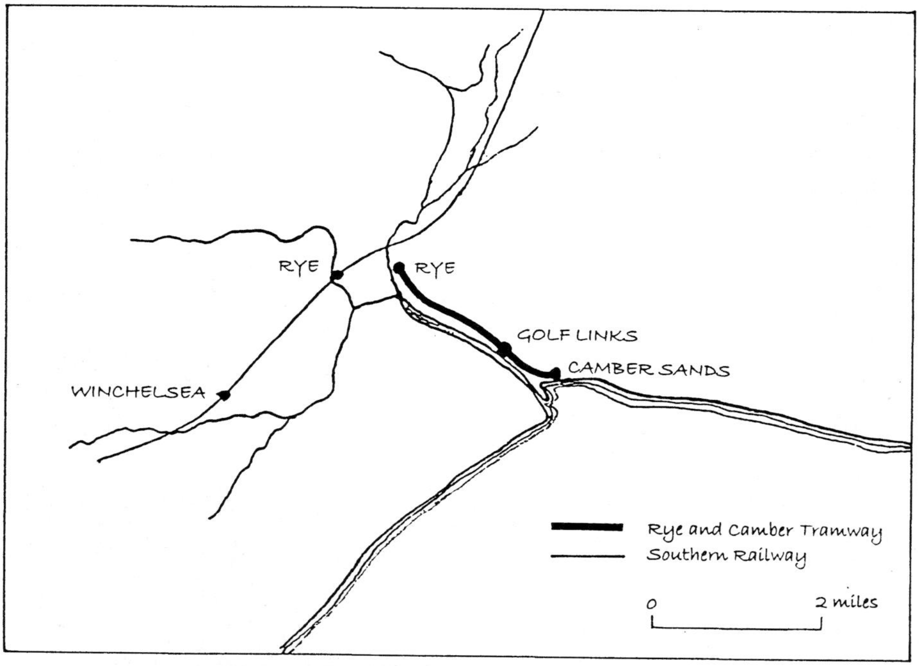

This 3ft gauge line was opened in 1895 from Rye on the south coast of England to the golf club at Camber, $1^1/_2$ miles to the south. At this time there was very little on the sandbanks at Camber except the golf club. A half-mile extension to Camber Sands was opened in 1908.

The first train that ran in 1895 was hauled by a 2-4-0T locomotive, *Camber*, built by Bagnall, no.1461. There followed in 1897 a second 2-4-0T named *Victoria*, also built by Bagnall, no.1511.

In 1925, Colonel Stephens, who was Engineer of the tramway, introduced a petrol locomotive built by the Kent Construction Co. of Ashford. This proved very successful and was modified and improved during the years; and when I visited the tramway, it seemed to be responsible for most of the traffic (figure 1.32). *Victoria* was withdrawn when the petrol engine arrived, and cannibalised for spare parts for *Camber*. This was the only steam engine I was able to photograph, poking her nose out of the shed (figure 1.31).

Figure 1.31 2-4-0T, *Camber*, Bagnall no.1461 of 1895.

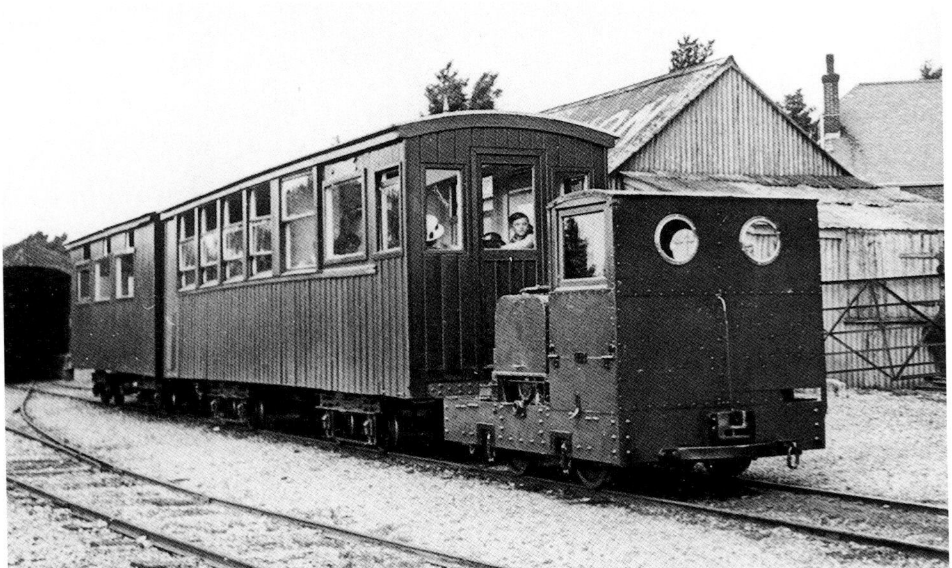

Figure 1.32 The petrol engine and train at Rye.

The tramway was still operating at the outbreak of war in 1939 when requisitioned by the Admiralty. After the war was over, the tramway was returned to the owners; but as the track and rolling stock was in such a neglected state, it was decided to wind up the company. By September 1967, the land leased from Rye Council was surrendered, and the track taken up shortly afterwards.

Chapter Two

South West

LYNTON AND BARNSTAPLE RAILWAY

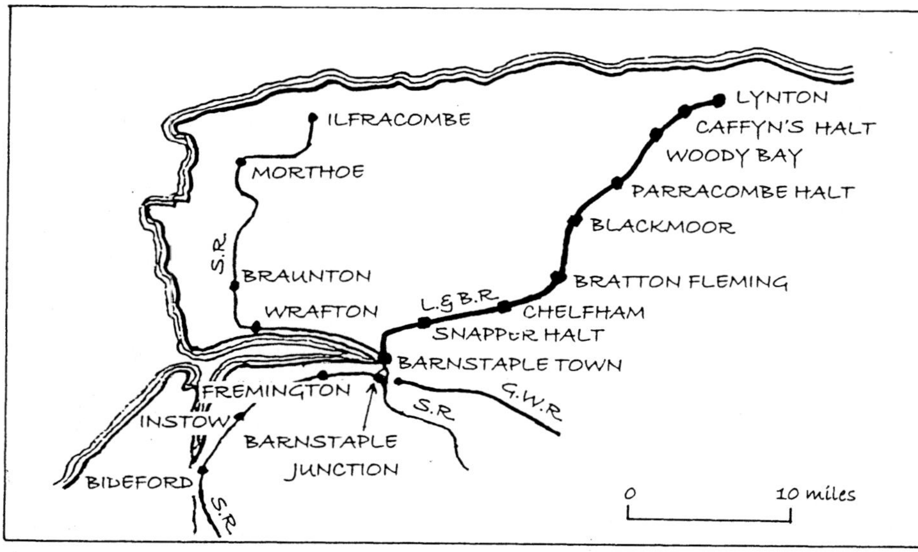

BARNSTAPLE TOWN and LYNTON and LYNMOUTH.

Down.	Week Days.								Sn.
	mn	mn	mrn	aft	aft	aft	JF	aft	aft
Barnstaple Town..dep.	533	7 0	1015	133	315	430	4A55	750	3AJ50
Snapper Halt..........	544	...	1026	144	326	441	....	8 1	....
Chelfham..............	552	.	1035	153	335	450	5C15	8 9	4CJ15
Bratton Fleming.......	6 6	731	1050	2 8	349	5 4	5 35	823	4J35
Blackmoor	623	749	11 8	226	4 8	522	5D55	841	4DJ55
Parracombe Halt.......	636	...	1121	240	423	536	6 3	855	5 J 3
Woody Bay.............	644	.	1130	250	432	245	6 8	9 3	5 J 8
Caffyns Halt..........	652	...	1139	259	441	553	..	911	..
Lynton & Lynm'th arr.	7 0	821	1148	3 8	450	6 2	6B25	920	5BJ25

Up.	Week Days.								Suns.	
	mn	mrn	aft	J	aft	aft	aft	aft	mrn	aft
Lynton & Lynm'th dep	713	9 25	1242	2B 0	330	612	8 5	9 30	9BJ30	1BJ45
Caffyns Halt	...	9 33	1250	....	338	620	813	9 38	....	....
Woody Bay.............	727	9 40	1257	2 17	345	627	820	9 45	9J47	2 J 2
Parracombe Halt.......	735	9 48	1 5	2 22	353	636	828	9 54	9J52	2 J 7
Blackmoor	749	10 2	1 19	2D30	4 7	650	841	10 7	10DJ0	2DJ15
Bratton Fleming	8 7	1020	1 37	2 50	425	7 8	858	1025	10J20	2J35
Chelfham..............	820	1034	1 51	3C10	448	722	912	1038	10CJ40	2CJ55
Snapper Halt.[176,177	829	1044	2 2	....	5 0	730	920	1047	....	....
Barnstaple Tn. G arr	841	1056	2 16	3A30	512	742	932	1059	11AJ0	3AJ1

A Barnstaple Junc. Sta. B Southern National Omnibus Office. C Chelfham Cross. D Blackmore Gate. F Fris. & Sats.
G Over ¼ mile to Barnstaple Sta. J or J By Southern National Motor Omnibus.

This was one of the finest narrow-gauge railways in Britain. Built on the 2ft gauge, the railway ran nineteen miles from Barnstaple, on the L.S.W.R. line to Illfracombe, and across the high land to Lynton on the North Devon coast.

For the opening in 1898 Manning Wardle supplied three large 2-6-2T. These were designed to deal with the many steep gradients found in both directions, and were among the most powerful ever built on this gauge. After the first year's successful traffic, another locomotive was purchased, this time a 2-4-2T from Baldwin of Philadelphia.

In 1923, as a result of the Grouping, the Lynton and Barnstaple Railway was taken over by the Southern Railway. They spent money on various improvements, including buying another Manning Wardle 2-6-2T.

In August 1931, on my first visit to Barnstaple, I found the narrow gauge train standing at the interchange platform. This was headed by No.759 *Yeo* (figure 2.1) looking very smart in bright Southern green with a polished brass dome, at the front of a mixed train including unusually capacious narrow-gauge carriages.

Figure 2 1 2-6-2T No.759 *Yeo* on train in the bay at Barnstaple Town.

I then walked a few hundred yards to Pilton shed where I found another fascinating subject: the Baldwin 2-4-2T was standing there, which I believed was unique (figure 2.2), being the only American built locomotive on the Southern Railway.

When I returned to Barnstaple Town's Station I was able to photograph another of the 2-6-2 tank engines, No.188 *Lew.* I also photographed one of the green passenger coaches (figures 2.3 and 2.4).

Figure 2.2 2-4-2T No.762 *Lyn* at Pilton shed.

Figure 2.3 2-6-2T No.188 *Lew* at Barnstaple Town.

Figure 2.4 Passenger coach at Barnstaple Town.

List of Lynton and Barnstaple Railway Locomotives.

No.188 2-6-2T *Lew* Manning Wardle no.2042 of 1925.
No.759 2-6-2T *Yeo* Manning Wardle no.1361 of 1897.
No.760 2-6-2T *Exe* Manning Wardle no.1362 of 1897.
No.761 2-6-2T *Taw* Manning Wardle no.1363 of 1897.
No.762 2-4-2T *Lyn* Baldwin no.15965 of 1898.

In spite of the encouraging support from the Southern Railway it was found that the line was not making a profit, and in 1935 it was decided to close the railway. Figure 2.5 shows the advertisement for the Dismantlement Sale.

All the older locomotives were cut up on the spot, but the most recent one, *Lew*, managed to escape to South America where it is believed she found work in a coffee plantation in Brazil.

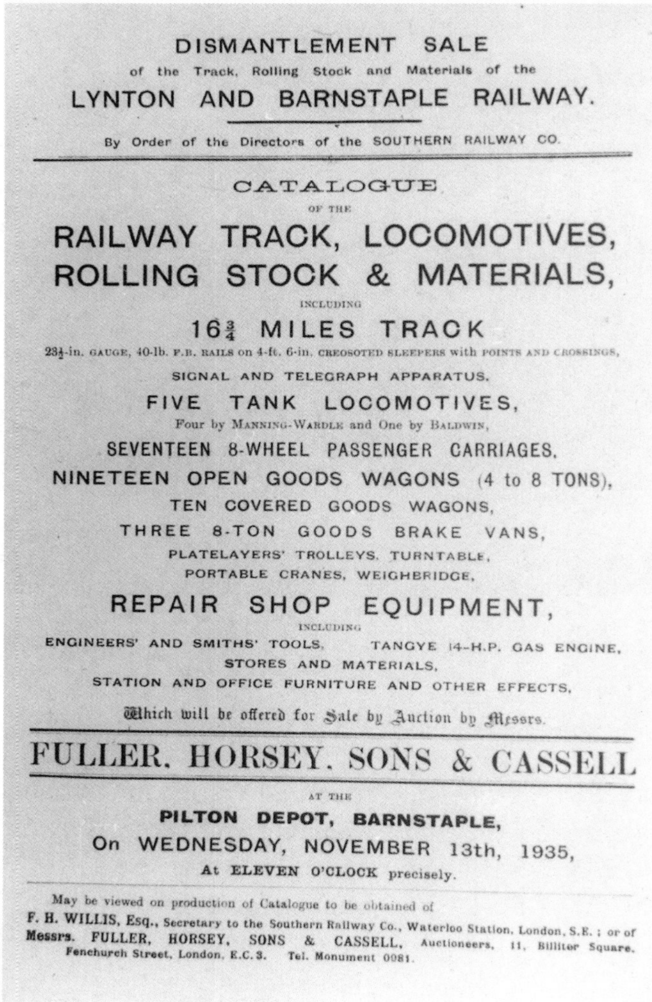

DISMANTLEMENT SALE
of the Track, Rolling Stock and Materials of the
LYNTON AND BARNSTAPLE RAILWAY.

By Order of the Directors of the SOUTHERN RAILWAY CO.

CATALOGUE
OF THE
RAILWAY TRACK, LOCOMOTIVES,
ROLLING STOCK & MATERIALS,
INCLUDING
$16\frac{3}{4}$ MILES TRACK
$23\frac{1}{2}$-in. GAUGE, 40-lb. F.B. RAILS on 4-ft. 6-in. CREOSOTED SLEEPERS with POINTS AND CROSSINGS,
SIGNAL AND TELEGRAPH APPARATUS.
FIVE TANK LOCOMOTIVES,
Four by MANNING-WARDLE and One by BALDWIN,
SEVENTEEN 8-WHEEL PASSENGER CARRIAGES.
NINETEEN OPEN GOODS WAGONS (4 to 8 TONS),
TEN COVERED GOODS WAGONS,
THREE 8-TON GOODS BRAKE VANS,
PLATELAYERS' TROLLEYS. TURNTABLE,
PORTABLE CRANES, WEIGHBRIDGE,
REPAIR SHOP EQUIPMENT,
INCLUDING
ENGINEERS' AND SMITHS' TOOLS, TANGYE 14-H.P. GAS ENGINE,
STORES AND MATERIALS,
STATION AND OFFICE FURNITURE AND OTHER EFFECTS,
Which will be offered for Sale by Auction by Messrs.

FULLER, HORSEY, SONS & CASSELL

AT THE
PILTON DEPOT, BARNSTAPLE,
On WEDNESDAY, NOVEMBER 13th, 1935,
At ELEVEN O'CLOCK precisely.

May be viewed on production of Catalogue to be obtained of
F. H. WILLIS, Esq., Secretary to the Southern Railway Co., Waterloo Station, London, S.E.; or of Messrs. FULLER, HORSEY, SONS & CASSELL, Auctioneers, 11, Billiter Square, Fenchurch Street, London, E.C.3. Tel. Monument 0081.

Figure 2.5 Notice of Dismantlement Sale, Lynton and Barnstaple Railway.

WESTON CLEVEDON AND PORTISHEAD LIGHT RAILWAY

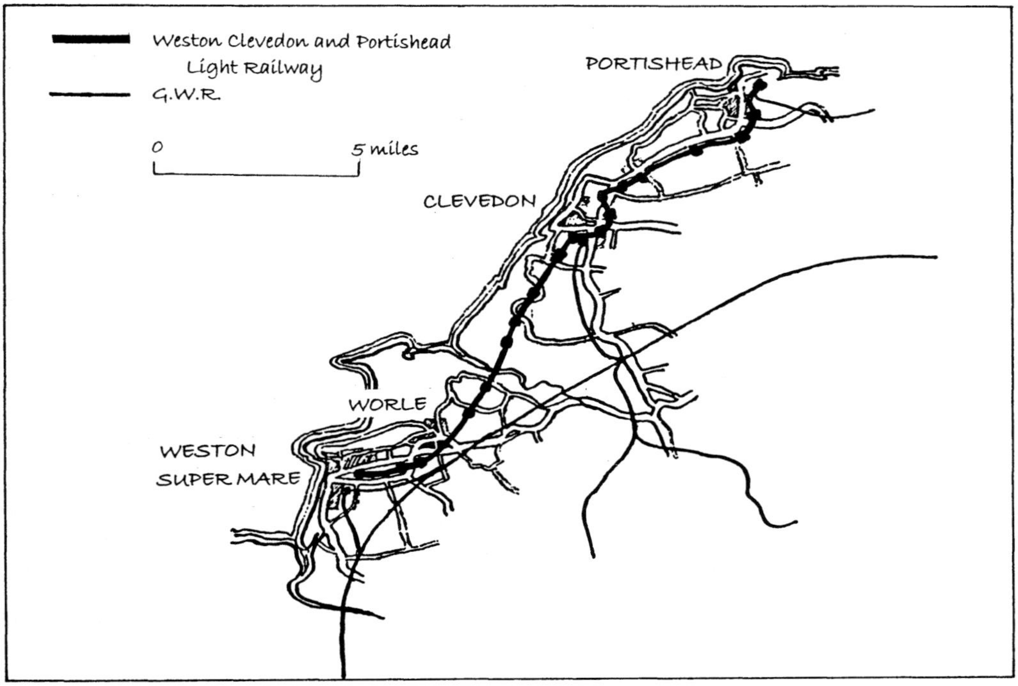

WESTON-SUPER-MARE and PORTISHEAD.—Weston, Clevedon, and Portishead.

Miles.	Up.	Week Days. mrn	mrn	non	aft	aft (Except Wednesdays)	aft	aft	Sundays. mrn
	Ashcombe Road Station, **Weston-super-Mare** ....dep.	9 0	1047	12 0	3 0	4 30	6 0	8 3	9 15
1	Milton Road	**Aa**	**Aa**	**Aa**	**Aa**	**Aa**	**Aa**	**Aa**	**Aa**
1½	Bristol Road	9 6	1053	12 6	3 6	4 33	6 6	8 9	9 21
2	Worle Town	9 9	1056	12 9	3 9	4 36	6 10	8 12	9 24
3¼	Ebdon Lane	**Aa**	**Aa**	**Aa**	**Aa**	**Aa**	**Aa**	**Aa**	**Aa**
4	Wick St. Lawrence	9 17	11 4	1217	3 17	4 44	6 18	8 19	9 31
5	Ham Lane	9 21	11 8	1221	3 21	4 48	6 22	8 23	**Aa**
5¾	Broadstone	**Aa**	**Aa**	**Aa**	**Aa**	**Aa**	**Aa**	**Aa**	**Aa**
6¾	Kingston Road	9 24	1111	1224	3 25	4 51	6 25	8 27	9 38
7¼	Colehouse Lane	**Aa**	**Aa**	**Aa**	**Aa**	**Aa**	**Aa**	**Aa**	**Aa**
8¼	**Clevedon F 47**	9 35	1117	1230	3 30	5 0	6 30	8 32	9 45
9	Clevedon East	9 38	..	1233	3 32	..	6 33	..	..
9¼	Clevedon (All Saints')	9 39	..	1234	3 33	..	6 34	..	..
9¾	Walton Park	**Aa**	..	**Aa**	**Aa**	..	**Aa**	..	..
10¼	Walton-in-Gordano....[dano)	9 43	..	1238	3 37	..	6 38	..	..
11¼	Cadbury Rd. (Walton-in-Gor-	9 47	..	1242	3 41	..	6 42	..	..
13	Clapton Road	**Aa**	..	**Aa**	**Aa**	..	**Aa**	..	..
13¾	Portishead Sth. (Portboy Rd.)	9 51	..	1246	3 45	..	6 46	..	..
14¼	**Portishead J 45** ....arr.	10 0	..	1 0	4 0	..	6 52	..	..

Aa Stops when required. **F** Adjoining Great Western Station. **J** ½ mile to Great Western Station.

This standard gauge light railway was opened in 1907 running 14¼ miles from Weston-super-Mare to Portishead. In 1911 the manager retired and was succeeded by Colonel Stephens who started to make changes by buying various second-hand locomotives.

On my first visit I walked up to the station and found that my train to Clevedon was to be a modern looking Drewry railcar. This was painted in Southern Railway colours and I discovered that it had only recently arrived from there where it had been undergoing trials (figure 2.6). I had a comfortable ride to Clevedon, very different from the one I had previously experienced when I travelled on the Ford railcar of the Selsey Tramway.

Figure 2.6 Drewry railcar at Weston-super-Mare.

On arrival at Clevedon I was able to photograph three locomotives. Just visible in the shed was 2-4-0T, No.1 *Clevedon*, built by Dubs & Co. no.1272 of 1879, formerly of the Jersey Railway (figure 2.7).

0-6-0T, No.2 *Portishead*, was an ex L.B.S.C. Stroudley Terrier, formerly No.643 with a train of four-wheeled carriages. Those at the head of the train were ex L.S.W.R, followed by ex Metropolitan Railway carriages (figure 2.8).

The third engine was 0-6-0ST, No.5, built by Manning Wardle, no.1970 of 1919. On later visits I discovered she was responsible for most of the work on this line. This engine had unusual solid driving wheels, specifically ordered by Colonel Stephens. Views of No.5 are shown in figures 2.9 and 2.10.

Figure 2.7 2-4-0T, No.1 *Clevedon*, Dubs & Co. no.1272 of 1879, ex Jersey Railway.

Figure 2.8 0-6-0T, No.2 *Portishead*, ex L.B.S.C Terrier, no.643.

Figure 2.9 0-6-0ST, No.5, Manning Wardle no.1970 of 1919.

Figure 2.10 No.5 on train at Clevedon.

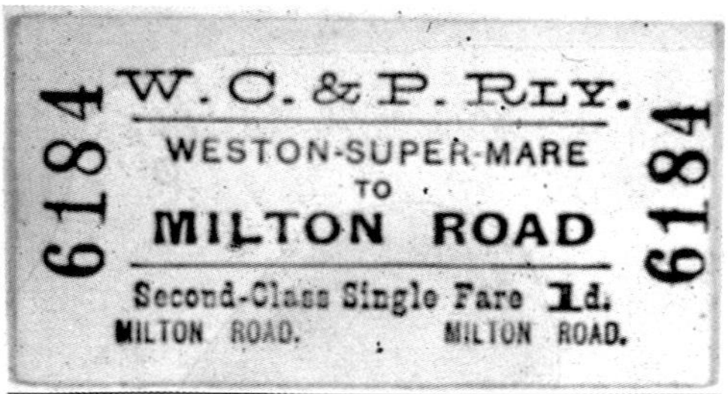

Two Weston Clevedon and Portishead Light Railway tickets.

The railway closed in 1940. No.5, the Manning Wardle, was scrapped, and the Terrier No.2, together with another Terrier, W.C.& P.R. No.4, were taken over by the Great Western Railway and became their Nos. 5 and 6. By chance I was able to photograph number 6 at Swindon in 1948 (figure 2.11).

Figure 2.11 Former W.C.& P.R. No.4, seen at Swindon in May 1948 as Great Western No.6.

Chapter Three

Wales

CORRIS RAILWAY

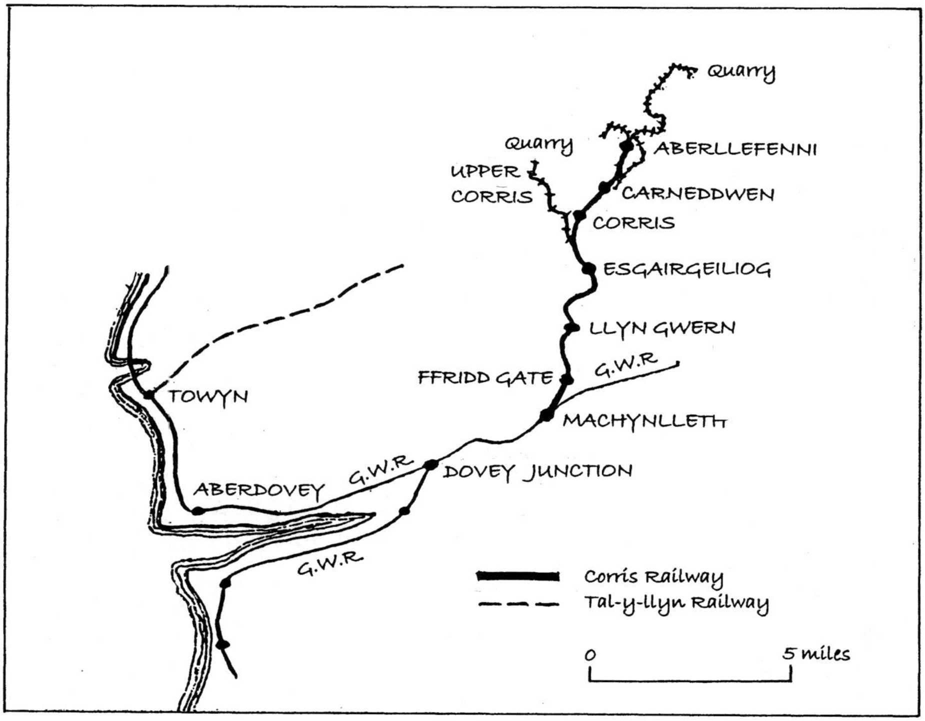

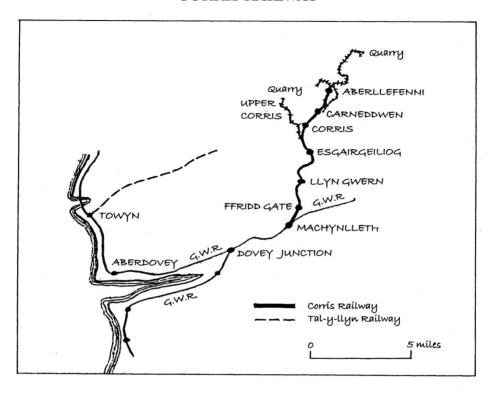

Originally this 2ft 3in gauge railway was the Corris, Machynlleth and River Dovey Tramroad opened in 1859 to deal with the slate traffic. At first it was operated by horses, but in 1864 it was renamed the Corris Railway to be operated by steam locomotives hauling passenger coaches.

The three original locomotives were 0-4-0ST and carried plates from the Falcon Engineering and Car Works numbers 324, 322 and 323 of 1878. These builders plates were misleading, as the locomotives had all been built by Henry Hughes & Co.; and when this firm had converted the engines to 0-4-2ST, it had already become the Brush Electrical Engineering Co. Ltd.

No.1 and No.2 were scrapped in 1930, but an 0-4-2ST was supplied new from Kerr Stuart, no.4047 in 1921, becoming number 4.

In 1930 the Corris Railway was taken over by the Great Western Railway and the passenger services closed at the end of that year. Transport of slate and other goods continued until the line closed in 1948.

When a school friend and I went to visit the Corris Railway in July 1933 we travelled on the Great Western Railway behind a Duke class 4-4-0 to Machynlleth station. Here we found Corris No.4 shunting (figures 3.1, 3.2).

Figure 3.1 Corris Railway No.4 shunting at Machynlleth.

Figure 3.2 Another view of Corris Railway No.4.

As there were no passenger trains we decided to start walking north along the Corris route to see what we could find and possibly to penetrate as far as the Tal-y-Llyn Railway.

This turned out to be a fascinating walk. For the first five miles we travelled along a deep twisting wooded river valley and for most of the way the railway track was close to the road, separated only by a fence. After passing little villages and the works at Corris we came to open country at the Tal-y-Llyn Lake beneath Cader Idris. The next day we were well placed to investigate the Tal-y-Llyn Railway.

TAL-Y-LLYN RAILWAY

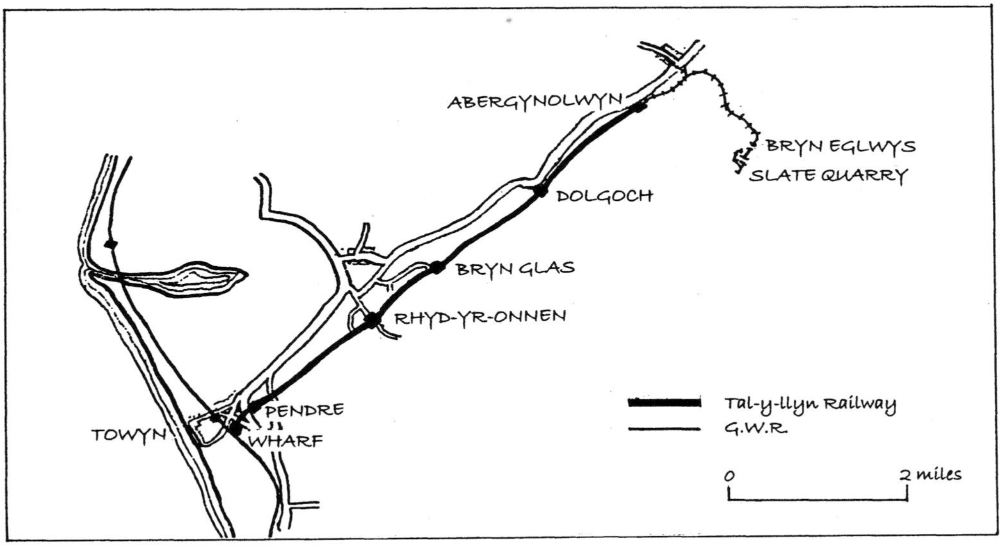

TOWYN and ABERGYNOLWYN.—Tal-y-llyn.

Miles.	Up.	Mons. only. mrn b		mrn		aft	aft	
	Towyn (Wharf)....dep.		..	9 25	..	2 15	..	..
½	" (Pendre)	6 0	..	9 30	..	2 20	5 50	..
2¼	Rhydyronen...........	6 10	..	9 40	..	2 30	6 0	..
3¼	Brynglas..............	6 15	..	9 45	..	2 35	6 5	..
5	Dolgoch...............	6 25	..	9 55	..	2 45	6 15	..
7	**Abergynolwyn H** arr.	6 40	..	1010	..	3 0	6 30	..

Miles.	Down.	Mons. only. b		mrn		aft	aft	
	Abergynolwyn ...dep.	6 50	..	1120	..	4 0	6 35	..
2	Dolgoch................	7 5	..	1135	..	4 15	6 50	..
3½	Brynglas..............	7 15	..	1145	..	4 25	7 0	..
4½	Rhydyronen......{140	7 20	..	1150	..	4 30	7 5	..
6½	**Towyn** (Pendre) **J** ...	7 30	..	12 0	..	4 40	7 15	..
7	" (Wharf)....arr.	..	..	12 5	..	4 45	7 20	..

b Not when any stoppage occurs at Bryneglwys Quarries.
H Sta. for Cader Idris (6 mls.) & Tal-y-llyn Lake (3¾ mls.). **J** ½ mile to G.W. Station.

This 2ft 3in gauge railway was opened in 1865 from Towyn on the North Wales Coast to Abergynolwyn, seven miles inland.

When I made my first visit to this railway, a friend and I had walked over the hills from the Corris Railway and arrived at the inland terminus at Abergynolwyn where we stayed the night. In the morning we were disappointed to be told in the village that there would be no trains that day to Towyn. However, all the local people were very insistent that the normal thing to do was to climb up the cable-incline to Abergynolwyn station where we should push a slate wagon from the siding and just use gravity to take us all the way to Towyn at the bottom end of the line.

With the use of the handbrake and occasional pushing at the difficult bits (figure 3.3), we eventually reached the yard at Pendre Shed at Towyn. Here we met a man who said, in a matter-of-fact sort of way, 'That'll cost you one shilling'.

Figure 3.3 Gravity-driven wagon on the Tal-y-Llyn Railway.

The two locomotives purchased when the railway first opened were still here: 0-4-2ST (originally 0-4-0ST), No.1 *Tal-y-Llyn*, Fletcher Jennings no.42 of 1864, and 0-4-0WT, No.2 *Dolgoch*, Fletcher Jennings no.63 of 1866.

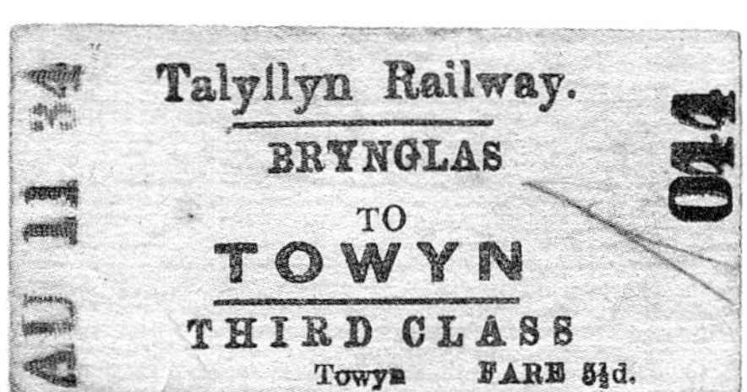

Third class railway ticket.

I photographed No.2 *Dolgoch* shunting at Towyn (figure 3.4), and another shot taken later in the day shows her resting, simmering in a rustic woodland scene (figure 3.5).

Figure 3.4 0-4-0WT, No.2 *Dolgoch* of the Tal-y-Llyn Railway.

Figure 3.5 Another view of No.2 *Dolgoch*.

In 1951 the railway was saved from closure by the Tal-y-Llyn Railway Preservation Society. The Tal-y-Llyn became the first railway to be rescued and operated by enthusiasts when, on 12th May 1951, Dolgoch set off from Towyn with a train of the original coaches. At the time of writing, this successful railway is approaching its fiftieth birthday since preservation.

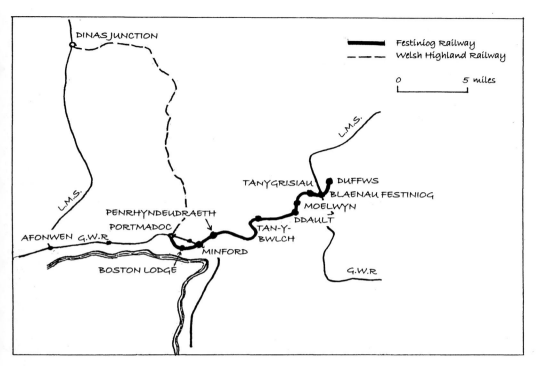

FESTINIOG RAILWAY

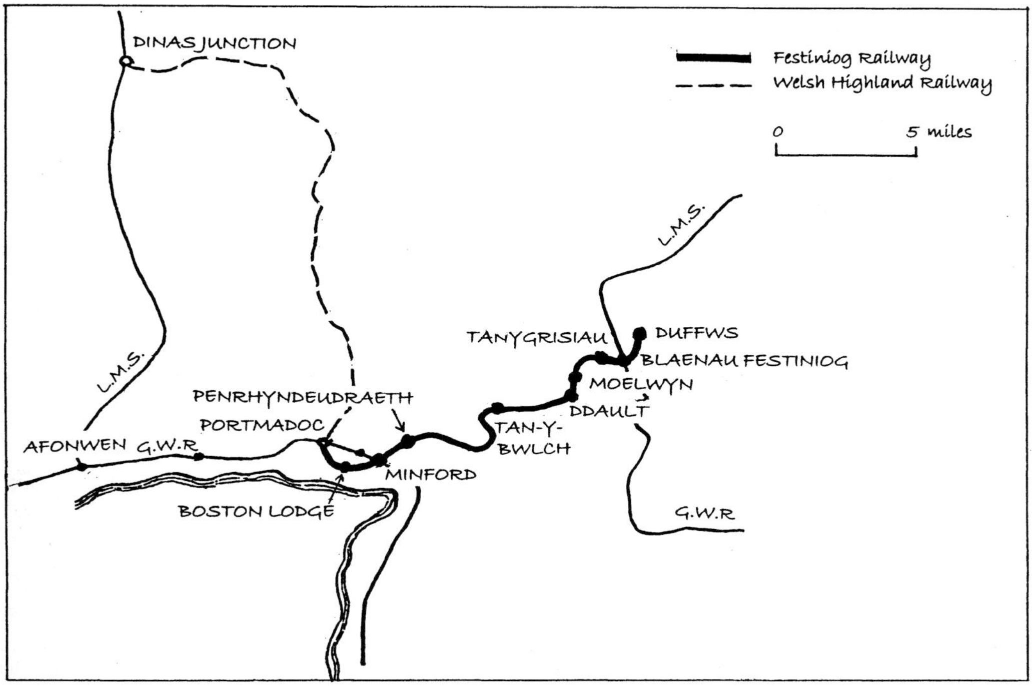

DINAS JUNCTION, PORTMADOC, BLAENAU FESTINIOG, and DUFFWS.—Festiniog and Welsh Highland.

Mls		mrn		mrn (Except Saturdays)		aft (Except Saturdays)
	Dinas Junction ....dep.					
2	Tryfan Junction					
3½	Waenfawr					
4¾	Bettws Garmon					
5½	Salem					
6	Plas-y-Nant					
7¼	Quellyn Lake					
9¼	**South Snowdon A** ... arr. / dep.					
10¼	Pitt's Head					
11¾	Hafod Ruffydd					
13¼	**Beddgelert** ... arr. / dep.					
15¼	Nantmor, for Aberglaslyn					
16¾	Hafod-y-Llyn					
17¾	Hafod Garregog					
18	Croesor Junction					
18¾	Ynysfor, for Llanfrothen					
19¾	Pont Croesor, for Prenteg					
21½	**Portmadoc** (N.) **B 140** arr. / dep					
21¾	" (Harbour)	5 15		10 15		3 10
22¾	Boston Lodge Halt **D**	Aa		Aa		Aa
24	Minffordd **140**	5 26		10 27		3 26
25¼	Penrhyndeudraeth **141**	5 31		10A32		3A31
29¼	Tanybwlch, for Maentwrog	5 54		10 55		3 54
31¼	Dduallt	Aa		Aa		Aa
32¼	Moelwyn Halt	Aa		Aa		Aa
33¼	Tanygrisiau	6 14		11A15		Aa
34¼	**Blaenau Festiniog 144, 504** L. M. S.	6 19		11 20		4 16
34¼	**Blaenau Festiniog** G. W.					
35	**Duffws** ....arr.					

Mls		mrn (Except Saturdays)		aft (Saturdays only)		aft (Except Saturdays)
	Duffws ....dep.					
	Blaenau Festiniog G. W.					
¾	**Blaenau Festiniog** L. M. S.	11 58		12 23		4 27
1½	Tanygrisiau	12 3		12A28		4A32
2¼	Moelwyn Halt	Aa		Aa		Aa
3½	Dduallt	Aa		Aa		Aa
5¼	Tanybwlch, for Maentwrog	12A23		12A48		4A52
9¼	Penrhyndeudraeth **141**	12A45		1A10		5A14
11	Minffordd **140**	12 52		1 17		5 21
12	Boston Lodge Halt **D**	Aa		Aa		Aa
13	**Portmadoc** (Harbour) **140**	1 2		1 27		5 31
13¾	" (New) **B**.. arr. / dep.					
15¾	Pont Croesor, for Prenteg					
16¾	Ynysfor, for Llanfrothen					
17	Croesor Junction					
17¾	Hafod Garregog					
18¾	Hafod-y-Llyn					
19½	Nantmor, for Aberglaslyn					
21¼	**Beddgelert** ... arr. / dep.					
23¾	Hafod Ruffydd					
24¾	Pitt's Head					
25¾	**South Snowdon A** ... arr. / dep.					
27¼	Quellyn Lake					
28¼	Plas-y-Nant					
29¼	Salem					
30¼	Bettws Garmon					
31¼	Waenfawr					
33	Tryfan Junction					
35	**Dinas Junction 514** ....arr.					

A 2¼ miles to the summit of Snowdon. A or **Aa** Stops when required. **B** Station for Borthygest; ¼ mile to the G.W. Station.
D For Portmeirion and Gwyllt Flower Gardens.

OTHER TRAINS between Portmadoc and Penrhyndeudraeth, see page 141.

This famous 1ft 11½in gauge Welsh railway was opened in 1836, originally as a horse tramway. Its pioneering development into an efficient steam-hauled railway was described in the railway literature of the time, so I already knew about the Spooner family of engineers and their vision of high-speed narrow-gauge trains hauled by powerful double Fairlie locomotives.

I had also read that in the early days the empty slate wagons had been drawn by horses for all of the thirteen miles of the railway. These wagons were then loaded at the Blaenau Festiniog slate quarries, seven hundred feet above sea level. The horses then mounted special carriages in which they rode with the loaded slate-wagons all the way back down to the sea.

I always hoped one day to see these horses riding in charge of the gravity-driven trains, but instead found high speed trains of bogie passenger carriages, hauled by double Fairlie locomotives.

Figure 3.6 shows one of these double Fairlie locomotives at the head of a passenger train about to leave Blaenau Festiniog on a journey down to Portmadoc on the coast.

Figure 3.6 0-4-4-0T, No.10 *Merddin Emrys* on train at Blaenau Festiniog.

Another view, also at Blaenau Festiniog shows 0-4-0ST, No. 5, *Welsh Pony* hauling slate trucks with one of the large tips in the background (figure 3.7). An older locomotive, No.4 *Palmerston* is shown in figure 3.8 and another view of *Welsh Pony* appears in figure 3.9.

Figure 3.7 0-4-0ST, No.5 *Welsh Pony* with a train of slate wagons at Blaenau Festiniog.

Figure 3.8 0-4-0ST, No.4 *Palmerston* at Portmadoc.

Figure 3.9 0-4-0ST, No.5 *Welsh Pony* with slate wagons.

Festiniog Locomotives at the time of my visits.

No.1	0-4-0ST	*Princess*	built by George England, 1863.
No.2	0-4-0ST	*Prince*	built by George England, 1863.
No.3	0-4-4-0T	*Taliesin*	built at Boston Lodge, 1885.
	(formerly No.11, *Livingston Thomson*).		
No.4	0-4-0 ST	*Palmerston*	built by George England, 1864.
No.5	0-4-0 ST	*Welsh Pony*	built by George England, 1867.
No.10	0-4-4-0T	*Merddin Emrys*	built at Boston Lodge, 1879.

The Festiniog Railway had well-equipped works at Boston Lodge at the far end of the embankment at Portmadoc.

There were, as I have previously mentioned, trains composed of comfortable bogie passenger carriages, but I also saw fascinating little four-wheel carriages, one of which can be seen next to the double Fairlie in figure 3.10. They had cramped back-to-back seating, and rather unusual "advice to passengers" which I was able to photograph (figure 3.11). The activities discouraged in this notice may appear rather irrelevant to a passenger in a modern railway coach, but seemed more excusable in these four-wheelers.

Figure 3.10 0-4-4-0T, No.3 *Taliesin* on train with four-wheeled coach.

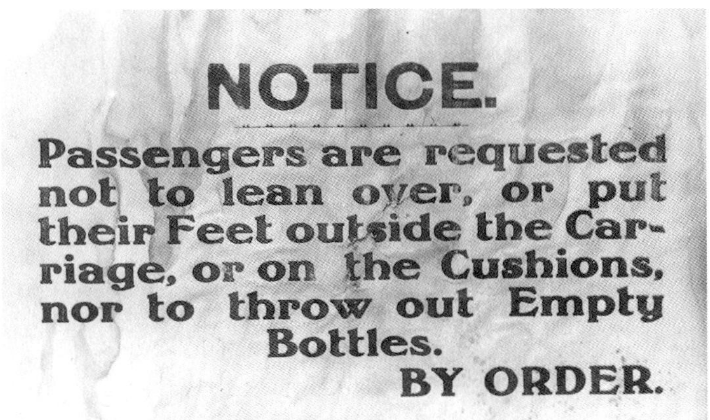

Figure 3.11 Notice to passengers.

The railway was in financial difficulties in the 1930s and the situation was not improved by its involvement with the neighbouring Welsh Highland Railway. The Festiniog Railway closed in 1943.

However this was not the end, and the railway reopened in 1955. After overcoming many difficulties it has now become very popular.

WELSH HIGHLAND RAILWAY

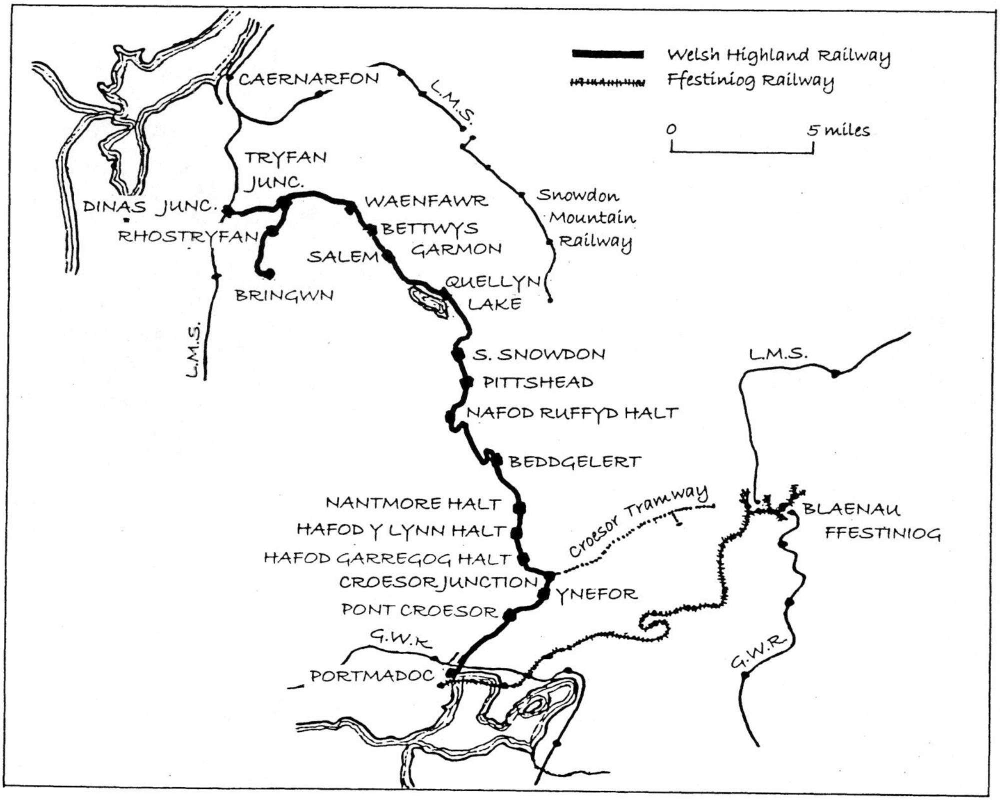

This railway originally ran between Dinas Junction, Caernarvon to South Snowdon in the wild country at the base of Snowdon, opening in 1881.

Many years later, the railway was extended and became the Welsh Highland Railway. This was done in stages to Croesor Junction, and partly over the track of the Croesor Tramway, to meet the Festiniog Railway at Portmadoc Harbour. The final section opened in January 1923.

When I made my visit in 1935 I discovered to my surprise that the line had been built across the Great Western Railway on the level in Portmadoc and ran across the High Street to a new station. It was good to be woken up in my bed-and-breakfast room by the sound of a locomotive just outside the window.

I took the train to Beddgelert where we met another train that had arrived from Dinas, drawn by *Russell*. Figure 3.12 shows *Russell* standing on the right and *Moel Tryfan* on the left ready to take the train back to Portmadoc.

Figure 3.12 *Russell* and *Moel Tryfan* at Beddgelert.

Welsh Highland Locomotives

2-6-2T	*Russell*	Hunslet no.901 of 1906.
4-6-0T	590	Baldwin no.45172 of 1917.
0-6-4T	*Moel Tryfan*	Amalgamation of Vulcan Foundry nos.738 and 739 of 1875.

Figure 3.13 0-6-4T single Fairlie *Moel Tryfan.*

Figure 3.14 2-6-2T *Russell.*

Figure 3.15 4-6-0T, No.590, built by Baldwin in 1917.

Figure 3.16 2-6-2T *Russell*. "We have a problem….."

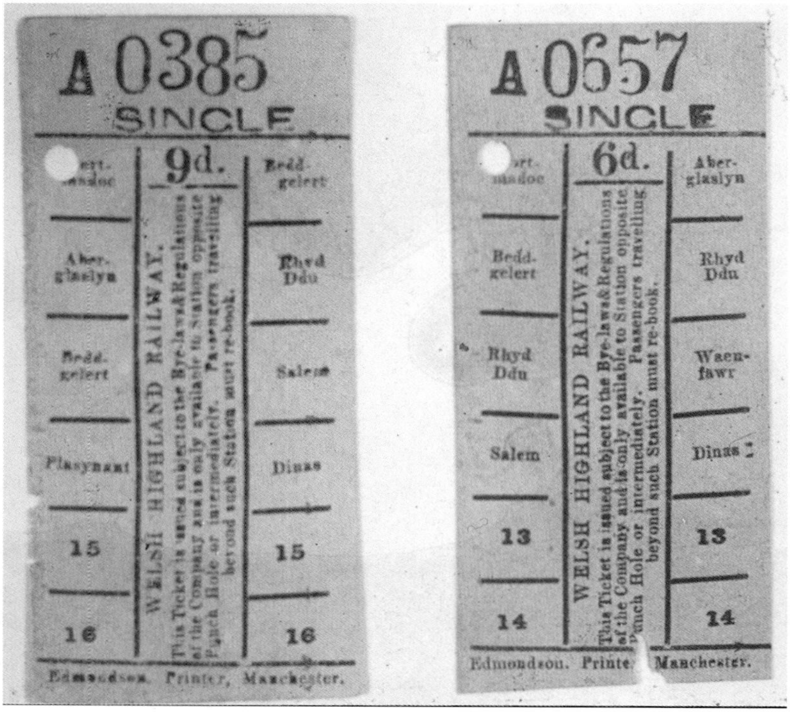

Welsh Highland Railway tickets.

The last passenger train ran on the Welsh Highland Railway in September 1936.

Attempts have been made by preservation societies to reopen the railway, and a major job involving much track laying is still in progress at the time of writing.

SNOWDON MOUNTAIN RAILWAY

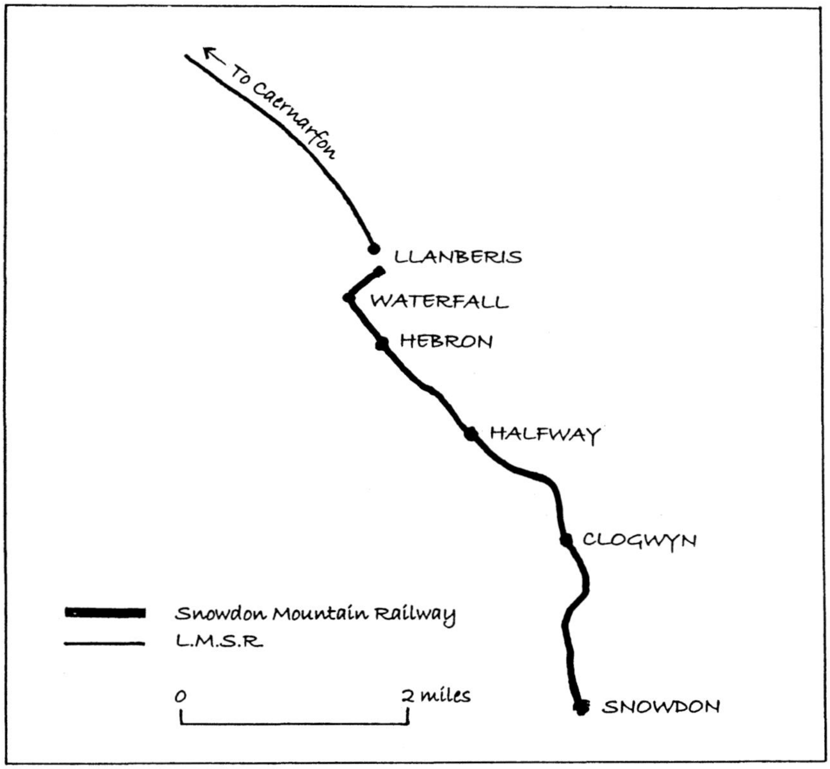

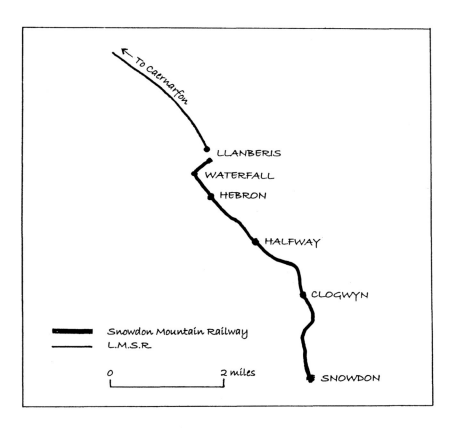

LLANBERIS and SNOWDON SUMMIT.—Snowdon Mountain.

Miles.	Week Days only.															
		mrn	mrn		non		A	aft	aft	A	aft	aft	aft	A	A	
	Llanberis ....dep.	7 30	1040	..	12 0	..	1230	1 0	1 30	2 0	3 0	3 30	4 0	4 30	5 0	..
1	Waterfall	..	..	...	..	..	..	..	..	..	..	..	..	..	..	..
2	Hebron	7 45	1055	..	1215	..	1245	1 15	1 45	2 15	3 15	3 45	4 15	4 45	5 15	..
3	Half Way	8 5	1110	..	1230	..	1 0	1 30	2 0	2 30	3 30	4 0	4 30	5 0	5 30	..
4	Clogwyn	8 23	1125	..	1245	..	1 15	1 45	2 15	2 45	3 45	4 15	4 45	5 15	5 45	..
5	**Snowdon Summit** .....arr.	8 40	1140	..	1 0	..	1 30	2 0	2 30	3 0	4 0	4 30	5 0	5 30	6 0	..

Miles.	Week Days only.															
		mrn	mrn		aft	A	aft	aft		A	aft	aft	aft	A	A	
	Snowdon Summit .....dep.	8 55	1155	..	1 30	2 0	2 30	3 0	..	3 30	4 30	5 0	5 30	6 0	6 30	..
1	Clogwyn	9 10	1210	..	1 45	2 15	2 45	3 15	..	3 45	4 45	5 15	5 45	6 15	6 45	..
2	Half Way	9 25	1230	..	2 0	2 30	3 0	3 30	..	4 0	5 0	5 30	6 0	6 30	7 0	..
3	Hebron	9 45	1245	..	2 15	2 45	3 15	3 45	..	4 15	5 15	5 45	6 15	6 45	7 15	..
4	Waterfall	..	..	..	..	..	..	..	..	..	..	..	..	..	..	..
5	**Llanberis 497a** ....arr.	9 55	1258	..	2 30	3 0	3 30	4 0	..	4 30	5 30	6 0	6 30	7 0	7 30	..

A Specials, and will only run as may be required.

No Trains will run with less than seven return Passengers, or the equivalent in Fares.

Trains will only run weather and other causes permitting.

The Snowdon Mountain Railway is unique in this country, as it has a rack-and-pinion track which enables trains to climb the steep gradients (1 in $5^1/_2$ at two places) to the summit of Snowdon at 3,500 feet. The total length is five miles and the gauge is 2ft $7^1/_2$in. The railway was opened in 1896 with 0-4-2T steam engines built in Switzerland.

List of Snowdon Mountain Railway Locomotives.

No.2	*Enid*	Winterthur no.924 of 1895.
No.3	*Wyddfa*	Winterthur no.925 of 1895.
No.4	*Snowdon*	Winterthur no.988 of 1896.
No.5	*Moel Siabod*	Winterthur no.989 of 1896.
No.6	*Padarn*	Winterthur no.2838 of 1922.
No.7	*Aylwin*	Winterthur no.2869 of 1923.
No.8	*Eryri*	Winterthur no.2870 of 1923.

No.1 does not appear on this list. On the opening day she was derailed near Clogwyn, plunged down the mountainside, and was damaged beyond repair.

My youthful view was that a steam railway was not an appropriate way to climb the highest mountain in Wales, so I never travelled on this line, preferring to reach the summit on foot. However, I overcame my prejudice and photographed some of the locomotives, both at the lower terminus and at the summit station (figures 3.17 and 3.18).

Figure 3.17 0-4-2T, No.2 *Enid* at Llanberis.

Figure 3.18 0-4-2T, No.6 *Padarn* at Snowdon summit.

With some assistance from diesel locomotives, this steam-powered railway continues to provide services which are still in great demand during the summer months.

VALE OF RHEIDOL LIGHT RAILWAY

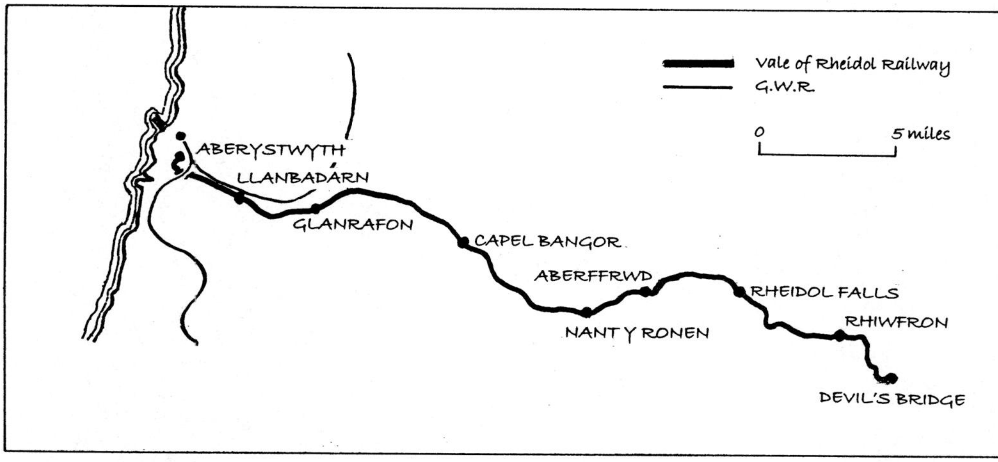

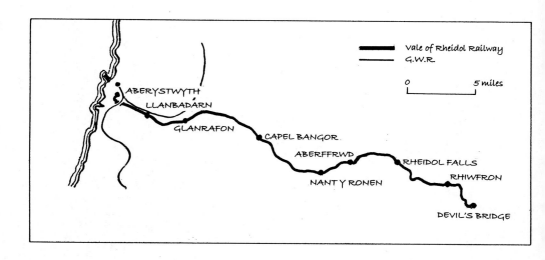

ABERYSTWYTH and DEVIL'S BRIDGE (One class only).

Miles	Up.	Week Days. mrn		Except Sats. aft	aft	Except Sats. aft		Sn aft
	Aberystwyth ..dep.	10 0	..	2 0	2 30	6 5	..	2 30
$4\frac{1}{4}$	Capel Bangor........	1020	..	2 20	2 50	6 25	..	2 50
$7\frac{1}{2}$	Aberffrwd..........	1032	..	2 32	3 2	6 40	..	3 2
$11\frac{3}{4}$	**Devil's Bridge**..arr.	11 0	..	3 0	3 30	7 10	..	3 30

Miles	Down.	Week Days. mrn	Except Sats. aft	aft	Except Sats. aft		Su aft
	Devil's Bridge..dep.	1130	4 15	5 45	7 30	..	5 30
$4\frac{1}{4}$	Aberffrwd...........	1154	4 39	6 9	7 54	..	5 54
$7\frac{1}{2}$	Capel Bangor ...[138	1211	4 56	6 25	8 12	..	6 11
$11\frac{3}{4}$	**Aberystwyth134** ar	1230	5 15	6 45	8 30	..	6 30

This 1ft $11\frac{1}{2}$ in gauge railway was $11\frac{3}{4}$ miles long and opened in 1902. Starting from Aberystwyth on the coast of Wales, the line ran up steep gradients into the mountains at Devil s Bridge. The railway was planned to serve lead mines, but later passenger services became more important.

The Cambrian Railways took over the line in 1912 followed by the Great Western Railway at the Grouping in 1923; but in spite of improvements made, the goods traffic was discontinued and the winter passenger service ceased. During the Second World War the line was closed and then British Rail took over in 1948. The railway had been in danger of closing in 1954, but efforts were made to keep it open with renewed publicity and new liveries and names for the remaining locomotives. These three locomotives, all 2-6-2T, were No.7 *Owain Glyndwr*, No.8 *Llywelyn* and No.9 *Prince of Wales.* Two were built at Swindon in 1923, but the *Prince of Wales* was built by Davies and Metcalfe Ltd in 1902.

I had missed this railway in my 1930s explorations and it was during this revival that I made my only visit to the line and took the photographs in figures 3.19 and 3.20, which are included for completeness.

Figure 3.19 No.8 and No.9 at Aberystwyth.

Figure 3.20 Train entering Devil's Bridge Station.

In 1964 the BR line to Carmarthen was closed, and during the following twenty years the Vale of Rheidol seems to have been steadily run down. In 1989 it was sold to a private company. After eleven years of consolidation, in the year 2000, it was once more running a flourishing passenger service.

WELSHPOOL & LLANFAIR LIGHT RAILWAY

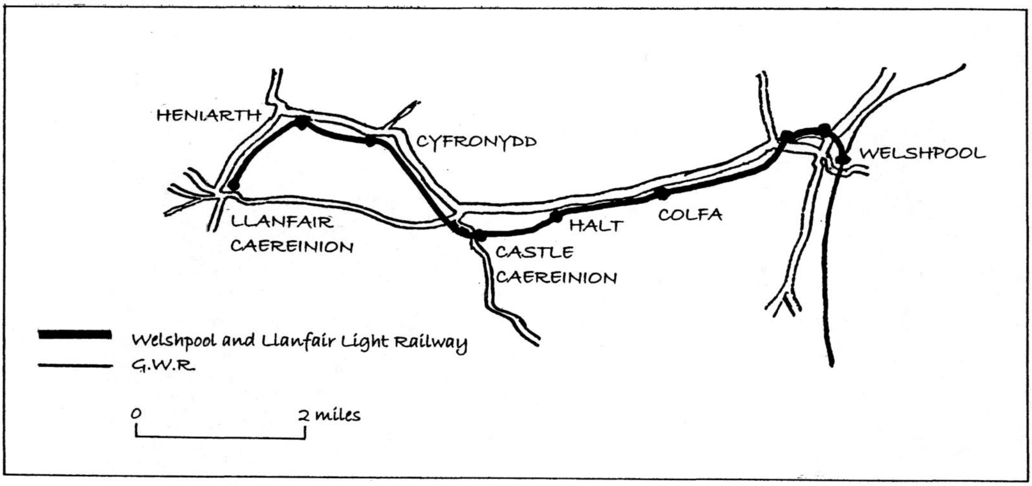

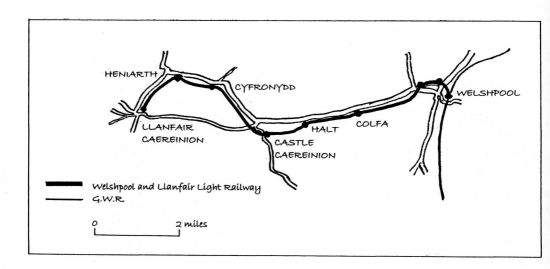

This 2ft 6in railway was opened in 1903 and ran for nine miles through farming country from Welshpool to the town of Llanfair Caereinion. The railway was opened under a Light Railway Order and it was arranged for the Cambrian Railways to work the line.

After the Cambrian Railways were merged with the Great Western, this line started a bus service over the route. It was found that this provided quicker services to Llanfair, and in 1931 the Great Western closed down the Light Railway to passengers.

When I visited this line, although there was no longer any passenger service, the two original locomotives could both be seen. These were 0-6-0T, *The Earl*, G.W.R. No.822, built by Beyer Peacock no.3496 of 1902, and 0-6-0T, *Countess,* G.W.R. No.823, Beyer Peacock no.3497 of 1902.

I photographed *The Earl* shunting at Welshpool, carrying the Great Western number plate (figure 3.21).

Figure 3.21 0-6-0T, *The Earl* at Welshpool.

For years after the railway had been closed to passengers, a flourishing goods service continued. However British Rail still closed the railway in 1956. Railway enthusiasts were determined to preserve the line and in 1960 the Welshpool and Llanfair Light Railway Preservation Company was formed. Both *The Earl* and *Countess* have been preserved in working order and many other locomotives have worked on this successful railway.

Chapter Four

Welsh Borders

BISHOP'S CASTLE RAILWAY

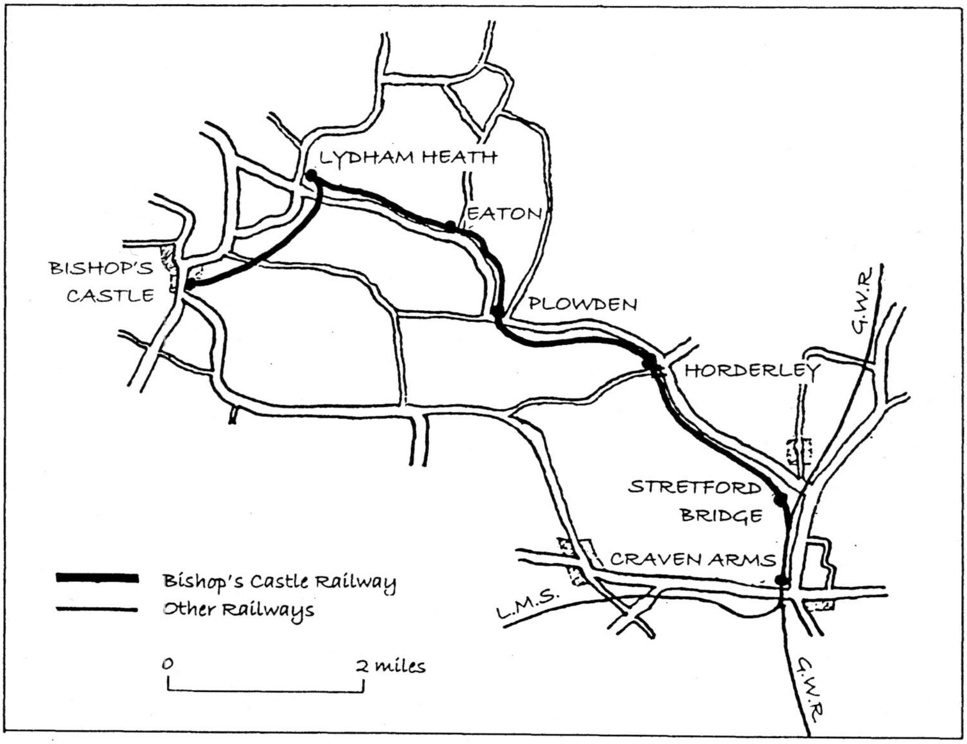

BISHOP'S CASTLE and CRAVEN ARMS AND STOKESAY.—Bishop's Castle.

Miles	Down.	Week Days only. mrn	Z	aft
	Bishop's Castle .... dep.	9 20	1240	5 30
2¾	Lydham Heath	9 30	1250	5 40
4	Eaton	Aa	Aa	Aa
5½	Plowden	9 45	1 10	5 50
7¼	Horderley	Aa	Aa	Aa
9¼	Stretford Bridge J. [486, 488	Aa	Aa	Aa
10½	Craven Arms & Stokesay arr	1015	1 30	6 20

Miles	Up.	Week Days only. mrn	Z	aft
	Craven Arms & Stokesay dep	1120	3 20	7 5
¾	Stretford Bridge Junction ...	Aa	Aa	Aa
3	Horderley	Aa	Aa	Aa
5	Plowden	1140	3 35	7 25
6½	Eaton	Cc	Aa	Aa
8¾	Lydham Heath	1153	3 48	7 35
10½	Bishop's Castle .... arr.	12 5	4 0	7 45

NOTES.

Aa Stop when required.
Cc Stops on Fridays only on notice being given to the Guard.
Z Mons., Fris., and Sats.

This 10½ mile standard gauge line in the Welsh border country was one of my special favourites. Opened in 1865, this railway had long been in financial difficulties and was eventually closed in 1935.

When I first arrived at Craven Arms Station, having travelled on the Great Western Railway, I found the Bishop's Castle train waiting for me in the bay. At the head was 0-6-0 *Carlisle*, built by Kitson in 1868, works no.1421 which had joined the Bishop's Castle Railway in 1895.

As we trundled along and turned off left at Stretford Bridge Junction, a rather unexpected thing began to happen. It had been raining hard and jets of water were shooting up through the floor due to the rather inadequate track ballast. This was something I had often come across in my bull-nosed Morris car, but it was the first time it had happened to me on a train.

Another unusual feature of the journey was the reversal of the railway at Lydham Heath. This was apparently due to over-ambitious plans to continue the line through Chirbury and thence to Minsterley or to Montgomery.

I stayed the night at Bishop's Castle at a bed-and-breakfast selected from the Cyclist Touring Club list. When I went to find the morning train for Craven Arms, I found the delightful sunny scene shown in figure 4.1.

Figure 4.1 0-6-0 *Carlisle*, ready to depart from Bishop's Castle.

Other Bishop's Castle subjects that I photographed on this day were an ex Great Western 0-4-2T, No.567, built in 1869 (figure 4.2), and a four-wheeled carriage (figure 4.3). The carriage was ex L.N.W.R. of 1860. One feature of this was its Clark and Webb's chain brakes, a design forbidden by the Board of Trade in 1924.

Figure 4.2 0-4-2T, No.567, ex Great Western Railway.

Figure 4.3 Four wheeled carriage, ex L.N.W.R.

My last two pictures were taken on 9th April 1936, exactly one year after the closure of the railway. I came across *Carlisle* backing off on a demolition train (figure 4.4), but conditions were not very good for photography, so the workers very kindly allowed me to drive *Carlisle* to a better place for photographs (figure 4.5). However they were not prepared to let me drive the engine back - I suppose in the fear that I might drive the train off the end of the Bishop's Castle Railway!

Figure 4.4 *Carlisle* hauling a demolition train.

Figure 4.5 *Carlisle*, after moving to a better photographic site.

Bishop's Castle Railway tickets.

GLYN VALLEY TRAMWAY

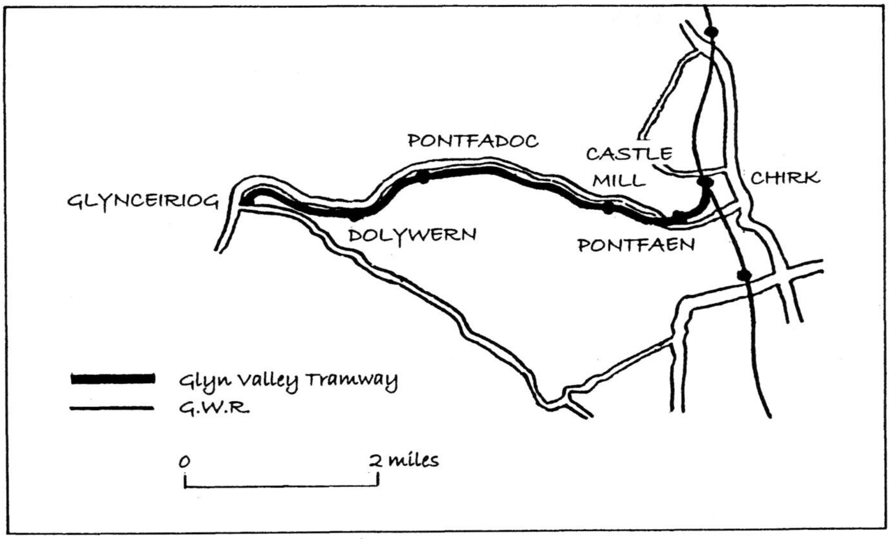

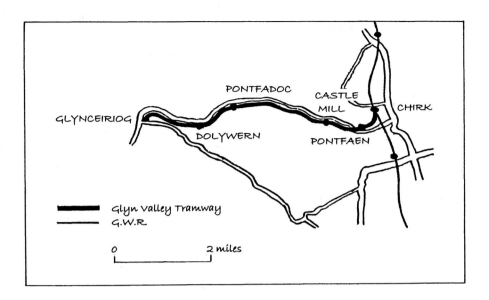

CHIRK, PONTFADOG, and GLYNCEIRIOG.—Glyn Valley.

Miles.	Up.	Wk Days only. mrn	aft	aft X	aft W	aft
	Chirk .... dep.	10 0	1 40	3 10	3 30	6 20
1¼	Pontfaen	Aa	Aa	Aa	Aa	Aa
2	Castle Mill	1011	1 51	3 21	3 41	6 29
4	Pontfadog	1023	2 3	3 33	3 53	6 40
5	Dolywern	1031	2 11	3 41	4 1	6 48
6½	Glynceiriog ...... arr.	1040	2 20	3 50	4 10	6 55

Miles.	Down.	Week Days only. aft		aft S		aft	aft
	Glynceiriog ...... dep.	1210	..	2 25	..	4 30	7 5
1½	Dolywern	1219	..	2 30	..	4 39	7 12
2½	Pontfadog	1227	..	2 41	..	4 47	7 19
4½	Castle Mill	1239	..	2 51	..	4 59	7 29
5¼	Pontfaen	Aa	..	Aa	..	Aa	Aa
6½	Chirk 108, 111 .... arr.	1250	..	3 0	..	5 10	7 44

Aa Stops when required.
S Sats. only.
W Weds. only.
X Except Weds.

The Glyn Valley Tramway was 2ft $4^1/_2$ in gauge and ran for eight miles from Chirk, on the Great Western Railway north of Shrewsbury to the mining village of Glyn Ceiriog. The Tramway was opened in 1891 when steam tram locomotives replaced the horses which had operated a local tramway up the valley in the Welsh border country.

The 1932 Bradshaw shows three trains had been running each way, but when I visited Chirk in 1933 the passenger service had just been suspended. However, I was able to see and photograph 0-4-2T, *Dennis* in steam in the yard (figures 4.6 and 4.7).

This was a great event for me as *Dennis* was the first steam tram locomotive I had ever seen. During my school days I lived in the western suburbs of London, and travelled everywhere by electric tram. This seemed to be the natural state of affairs, but my parents told me that there used to be trams hauled by horses. About 1900, horses were replaced by steam power, and for a few years, before electric trams were commonplace, steam tram engines were to be seen on the streets. Regulations compelled them to have working parts enclosed down to four inches above the ground. *Dennis* seemed to keep to these rules in every respect, and the Glyn Valley had three of these 0-4-2T tram engines.

Dennis, built by Beyer Peacock no.2970 of 1888
Sir Theodore, Beyer Peacock no.2969 of 1888
Glyn, Beyer Peacock no.3500 of 1892

Dennis was named after Henry Dennis, initially an engineer for the Tramway who became a Director. *Sir Theodore* was named after Sir Theodore Martin who was principal promoter of the Tramway, and Chairman for many years. There was also a Baldwin 4-6-0T no.45221, built in 1917 and modified by Beyer Peacock in 1921. The Baldwin did not seem very popular with the engine men who told me that I could take her away if I wanted!

Figure 4.6 0-4-2T, *Dennis*. The trains were usually hauled cab first.

Figure 4.7 Another view of *Dennis*.

Figure 4.8 A line of disused coaches at Chirk.

The Tramway was closed on 6 July 1935.

SHROPSHIRE AND MONTGOMERYSHIRE RAILWAY

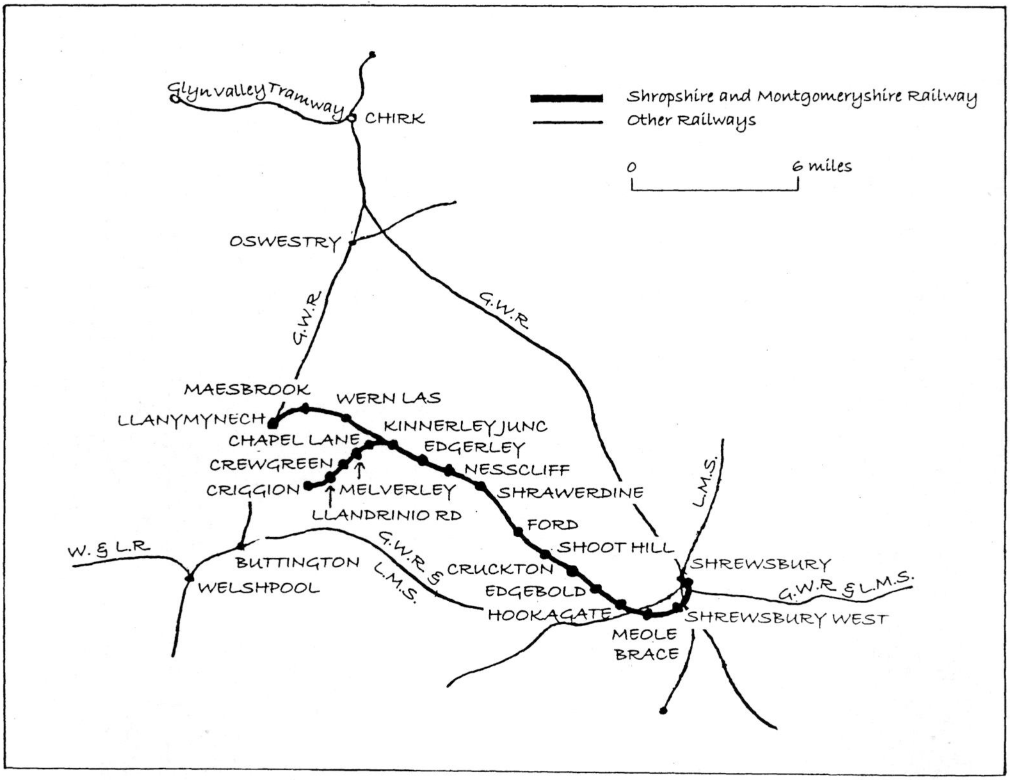

Shrewsbury and Llanymynech.] **1085**

SHREWSBURY, CRIGGION, and LLANYMYNECH.—Shropshire and Montgomeryshire.

Miles	Down.	mrn (Saturdays only.)	mrn	mrn	aft	aft (Saturdays only.)	aft	aft
	Abbey Station, Shrewsbury........dep.			9 40	1 45			6 20
1	Shrewsbury West			Cc	Cc			Cc
1½	Meole Brace			9 55	2 0			6 30
3	Hookagate and Redhill			Cc	Cc			Cc
4	Edgebold			Cc	Cc			Cc
5¼	Cruckton			Cc	Cc			Cc
6¾	Shoot Hill			Cc	Cc			Cc
7¾	Ford and Crossgates			1010	2 20			6 45
11¼	Shrawardine			Cc	Cc			Cc
13¾	Nesscliff and Pentre			1025	2 35			7 0
14½	Edgerley			Cc	Cc			Cc
15½	Kinnerley Junction		7 30	1035	2 45		4 30	7 10
—	Kinnerley Junc.dep.	7 25				3 0		
16½	Chapel Lane	Cc				Cc		
17¾	Melverley	7 35				3 10		
20¼	Crew Green A	Cc				Cc		
21¼	Llandrinio Road	7 45				3 20		
22¾	Criggion........arr.	7 50				3 25		
17	Wern Las		Cc	Cc			Cc	Cc
18	Maesbrook....[138,145		7 40	1050			4 40	7 20
20	Llanymynech 136, arr.		7 45	1055			4 45	7 25

Miles	Up.	mrn (Saturdays only.)	mrn	mrn	aft (Saturdays only.)	aft	aft
	Llanymynech......dep.		8 10	1125		5 0	7 35
2	Maesbrook		8 15	1130		5 5	7 40
3	Wern Las		Cc	Cc		Cc	Cc
— Mls	Criggion........dep.	8 0			3 30		
— 1	Llandrinio Road	8 5			3 35		
— 2	Crew Green A	Cc			Cc		
— 5¼	Melverley	8 15			3 45		
— 6¼	Chapel Lane	Cc			Cc		
— 7¼	Kinnerley Junc. arr.	8 25			3 50		
4½	Kinnerley Junction		8 35	1145		5 20	7 50
5½	Edgerley		Cc	Cc		Cc	
6¼	Nesscliff and Pentre		8 43	1155		5 28	
8¾	Shrawardine		Cc	Cc		Cc	
12¼	Ford and Crossgates		8 56	1210		5 40	
13¼	Shoot Hill		Cc	Cc		Cc	
14¾	Cruckton		Cc	Cc		Cc	
16	Edgebold		Cc	†Cc		Cc	
17	Hookagate and Redhill		Cc	Cc		Cc	
18½	Meole Brace		9 15	1230		6 0	
19	Shrewsbury West [488		Cc	Cc		Cc	
20	Shrewsbury B 486, arr.		9 30	1245		6 10	

NOTES.

A Station for Alberbury, Coedway.

B Abbey; about ½ mile to General Station.

Cc Stop when required.

The Shropshire and Montgomery Railway was opened under a Light Railway Order in 1911 on the site of a former railway which had been defunct for some years. This standard gauge line was under the management of Colonel Stephens and ran for twenty miles from Shrewsbury to Llanymynech, with a branch to Criggion.

When I visited the sheds and works at Kinnerley and took the photographs shown here, the passenger service had already ceased. The minimal service operating in the final year can be seen in the Bradshaw timetable.

At this time the railway owned four locomotives, the most unusual was 0-4-2WT *Gazelle*, built by Dodman of King's Lynn in 1893. This engine was originally a 2-2-2WT, but was converted to a 0-4-2WT for Colonel Stephens by W.G.Bagnall Ltd after she was purchased in 1911 for use as an inspection engine. At one time she used to haul an ex LCC horse tramcar on the Criggion branch, but when I saw her she was undergoing a heavy repair (figure 4.9).

Figure 4.9 0-4-2WT *Gazelle*.

It is good to know that W.H.Austen, the successor to Colonel Stephens, decided to have this engine completely overhauled again in 1936. She then ran occasional special passenger trips on the Criggion branch, hauling the old LCC tram. The next time I met her myself, she was on show at the Longmoor Military Railway. After that she went to the Museum of Army Transport at Beverley.

Like most of the railways of Colonel Stephens, this railway owned some Brighton Terriers, and the one I saw at Kinnerley was 0-6-0T No.9 *Daphne.*

Figure 4.10 0-6-0T No.9 *Daphne.*

Figure 4.11 0-6-0 No.6 *Thisbe.*

The Terriers do not seem to have been a success here. However the ex L.S.W.R. Ilfracombe Goods 0-6-0 tender engines were well suited to this railway which had purchased three. One had hauled the first train on the opening day. Two of them are shown in figures 4.11 and 4.12. No.3 *Hesperus* was built by Beyer Peacock, no.1517 of 1875, and was ex L.S.W.R. No.0324, while No.6 *Thisbe*, also built by Beyer Peacock, no.1209 of 1873 was ex L.S.W.R. No.0283.

Figure 4.12 0-6-0 No.3 *Hesperus.*

Figure 4.13 ex L.S.W.R. Royal Carriage.

The coach in figure 4.13 is an ex L.S.W.R. Royal Saloon. This was sometimes used as part of a train and required an extra fare supplement to travel in it.

Figure 4.14 is an unconventional one, showing myself standing on top of the boiler of *Thisbe* - presumably under the influence of pictures I had seen of hunters in darkest Africa standing on the prey they had shot!

The War Department took over the railway in 1941 and made extensive alterations and extensions. The line was finally closed in 1960.

Figure 4.14 'Successful hunter standing on his fallen prey'.

SNAILBEACH DISTRICT RAILWAYS

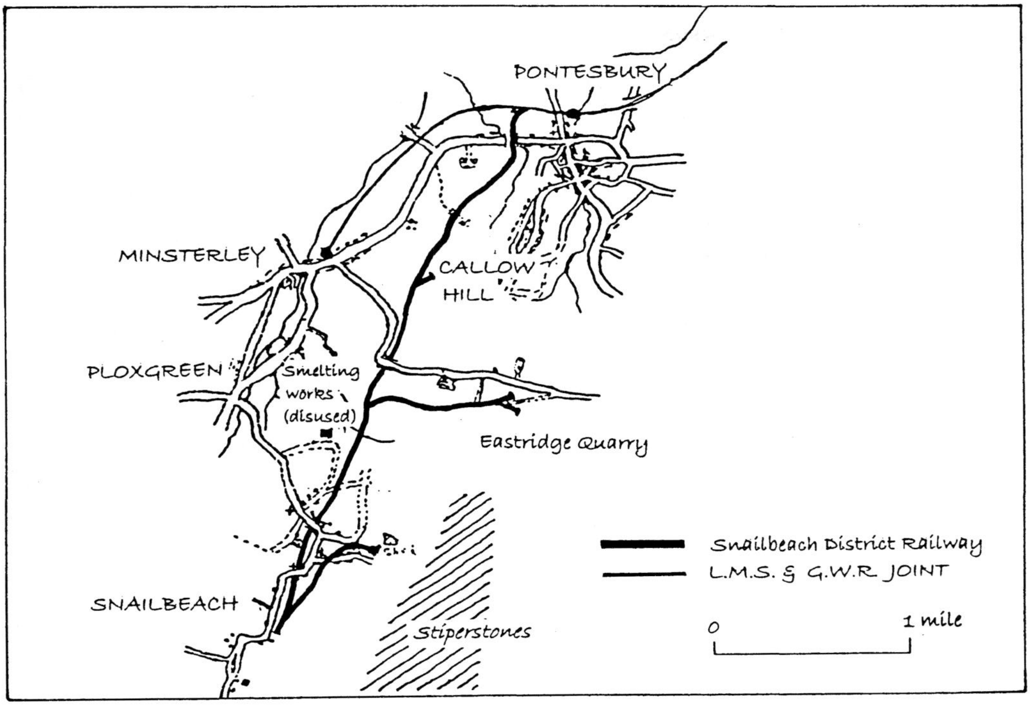

This 2ft 4in gauge railway was opened in 1877 and ran for three-and-a-quarter miles along the edge of the Stiperstones, south of Shrewsbury in the Welsh border country. Its purpose was conveying stone from some small mines to the main railway line at Pontesbury.

When I first visited this line I found 0-4-2T No.2, built by Kerr Stuart, no.802 of 1902 (figure 4.15) working near the shed at Snailbeach. Inside were two Baldwin 4-6-0Ts, built in 1916, works numbers 44383 and 44522. Behind the shed was 0-6-0T *Dennis* undergoing heavy repair (figure 4.15). This was built by Bagnall in 1906, works no.1797.

This engine was probably named after Sir Henry Dykes Dennis of Glyn Valley Tramway fame who was also the chairman of this railway. When Colonel Stephens took over the railway in 1923 he purchased the three locomotives that I had seen. They continued to work steadily until 1946, by which time they were completely worn out.

Figure 4.15 0-4-2T No.2, Kerr Stuart no.802 of 1902 of the Snailbeach District Railways.

Figure 4.16 0-6-0T *Dennis* lying behind the shed at Snailbeach.

In 1950, when the line had been closed for two years, the locomotives were all cut up at Snailbeach. I returned in that year just in time to see the remains of the last Baldwin. My photograph (figure 4.17) taken on 27th April 1950, shows the scene at the shed with the Stiperstones in the background.

Figure 4.17 Baldwin being cut up in 1950 on the Snailbeach District Railways.

Chapter Five

Central

EDGE HILL LIGHT RAILWAY

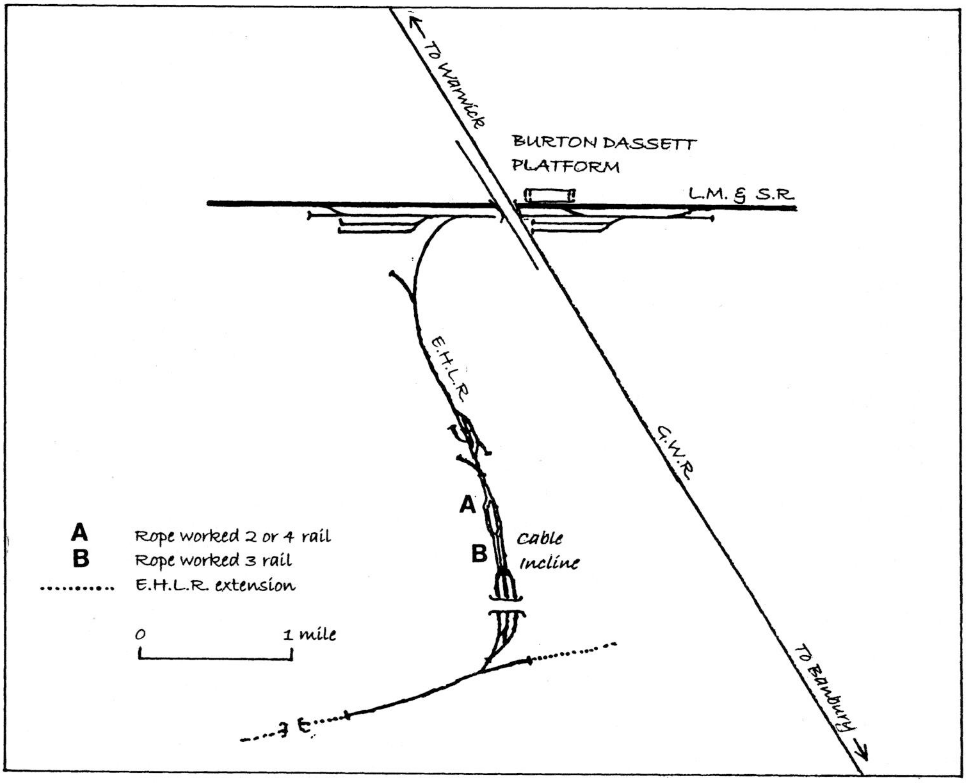

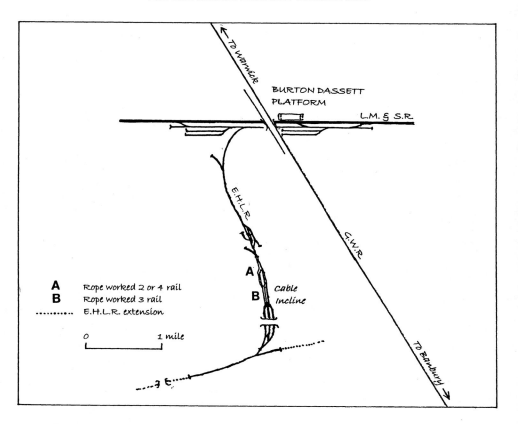

When I visited this railway in 1933 I came across a memorable sight. Standing not far apart were two silent trains of wagons, each headed by an ex-Brighton Terrier 0-6-0T. In addition a third locomotive stood at the top of a nearby cable incline, and this was a little Manning Wardle saddle tank engine. There was also an abandoned steam excavator with jib raised.

This scene of suspended animation made me think of the 'Marie Celeste' mystery of an abandoned sailing ship discovered at sea with all sails set and even the meals put out for the crew of whom no trace was ever found. I later discovered the railway had been abandoned some eight years before my visit, which explains why I did not find any cold mugs of tea left by the engine men!

The Edge Hill Light Railway was opened in 1919 on standard gauge and was less than four miles long. Beyond a level section there was an incline of 1 in 6 to reach the level of the iron-stone mines that the railway was designed to serve.

The three locomotives were 0-6-0T No.1, ex L.B.S.C. No.673, built at Brighton in 1872, 0-6-0T No.2, ex L.B.S.C. no.674, built in 1882, and 0-4-0ST, *Sankey* built by Manning Wardle, no.1088 of 1888.

Figure 5.1 0-6-0T No.2 abandoned with a train of wagons.

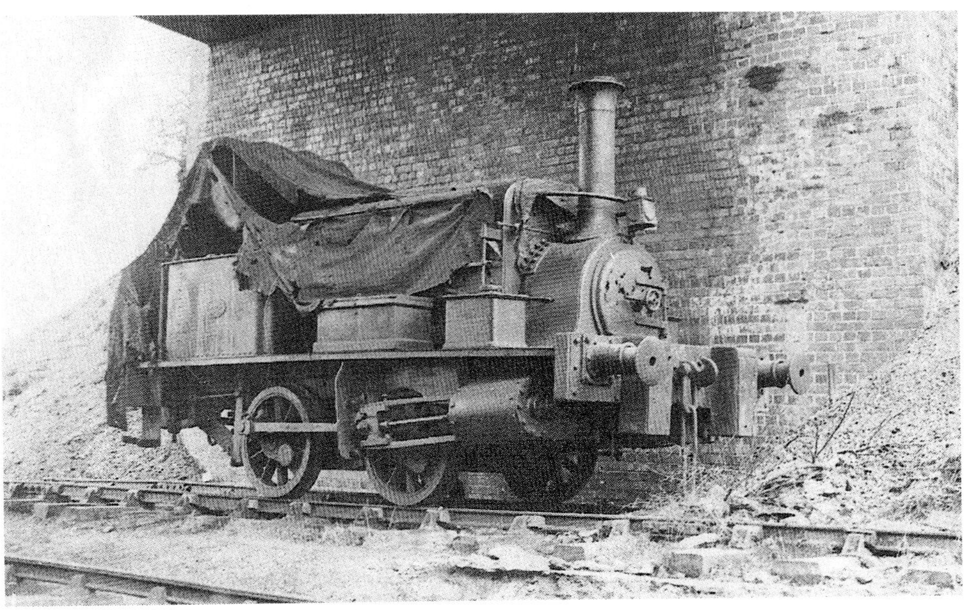

Figure 5.2 0-4-0ST *Sankey* under the bridge at the top of the incline.

The iron-ore trade declined and the last load came down the incline on 27th January 1925. On this day the railway apparently just stopped: the big steam excavator was left with its jib raised for the next scoop, and the two Terriers stood with their trains ready. The saddle tank engine *Sankey* remained at the top of the incline under a road bridge until twenty-one years later, in 1946, she and the two Terriers were cut up on the site.

ASHOVER LIGHT RAILWAY

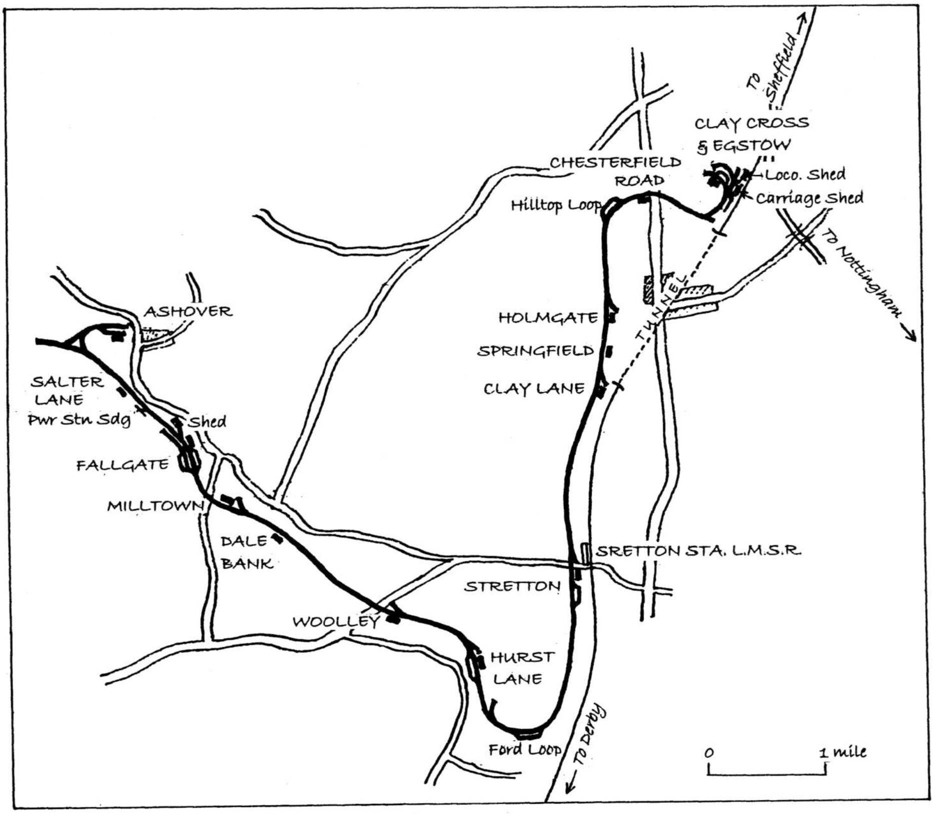

CLAY CROSS AND EGSTOW, STRETTON, and ASHOVER.—Ashover Light.

Miles	Up.	Weds. and Sats. mrn	mrn		aft	aft	aft	aft	aft		Sundays. aft	aft	aft
	Clay Cross H dep.	7 45	9 55	..	1215	2 45	4 50	7 0	9 15	..	2 45	5 0	7 10
½	Chesterfield Rd...	7 47	9 57	..	1217	2 47	4 52	7 2	9 17	..	2 47	5 2	7 12
2¾	Stretton 702, 703 arr.	7 59	1013	..	1231	3 1	5 6	7 16	9 31	..	2 58	5 13	7 23
	Stretton 702, 703 dep.	8 0	1014	..	1232	3 2	5 7	7 17	9 32	..	2 59	5 14	7 24
4¾	Woolley	8 13	1027	..	1245	3 15	5 20	7 30	9 45	..	3 12	5 27	7 37
6	Fallgate........	8 26	1040	..	1258	3 28	5 33	7 39	9 54	..	3 25	5 40	7 46
7¼	Ashover G..arr.	8 32	1046	..	1 4	3 34	5 39	7 45	10 0	..	3 31	5 46	8 0

Miles	Down.	Weds. and Sats. mrn	mrn		aft	aft	aft	aft	Sundays. aft	aft	aft
	Ashover G..dep.	8 38	11 0	..	1 30	3 45	6 0	8 15	3 45	6 10	8 15
1	Fallgate........	8 46	11 8	..	1 38	3 53	6 8	8 23	3 53	6 18	8 23
2½	Woolley	8 55	1117	..	1 47	4 2	6 17	8 32	4 2	6 27	8 32
4½	Stretton 702, 703 arr.	9 7	1127	..	1 57	4 12	6 27	8 42	4 12	6 37	8 42
	Stretton 702, 703 dep.	9 8	1128	..	1 58	4 13	6 28	8 43	4 13	6 38	8 43
6¾	Chesterfield Rd...	9 30	1150	..	2 20	4 35	6 50	9 2	4 35	7 0	9 2
7¼	Clay Cross H arr.	9 35	1155	..	2 25	4 40	6 55	9 5	4 40	7 5	9 5

G Ashover (Butts).

H Clay Cross and Egstow.

All Trains call at **Holmgate**, at **Springfield**, and at **Clay Lane**, between Chesterfield Road and Stretton; at **Hurst Lane**, between Stretton and Woolley; at **Dale Bank** and at **Milltown**, between Woolley and Fallgate; and at **Salter Lane**, between Fallgate and Ashover, when required.

The Ashover Light Railway was 2ft gauge, $7^{1}/_{4}$ miles long, and opened in 1925 to serve the Clay Cross Company, north of Derby. This company operated a large quarry which had a valuable contract to supply the L.M.S.R. with granite chips for track ballast.

In 1936, when I first visited this railway, I found a Baldwin 4-6-0T at Clay Cross with a couple of good-looking coaches (figure 5.3), but passengers seemed rather scarce.

Figure 5.3 4-6-0T *Hummy* on train.

Figure 5.4 4-6-0T *Hummy* at Clay Cross.

The locomotives were all 4-6-0T, built in the USA by Baldwin. The first four were obtained from the War Disposals Board in 1923, and a further two via T.W.Ward Ltd. The names and Baldwin numbers (of 1917) were:

Joan	44720
Peggy	44743
Hummy	45227
Guy (the first)	44370
Guy (the second)	44695
Bridget	44737

They were all named after the children of General Humphrey Jackson, at one time General Manager of the Clay Cross Company. The name *Hummy* referred to Henry Humphrey, General Jackson's second son. The second *Guy* appeared when it was found that putting the first *Guy* in order would be so expensive that it was cheaper to purchase another similar Baldwin as a replacement.

As all five engines were very alike in design, considerable exchange of parts and cannibalisation is known to have taken place. For example, at one time an engine was running with a tank from *Joan* on one side and a tank from *Bridget* on the other.

The line was closed to passengers in 1936, but the whole railway continued until 1960.

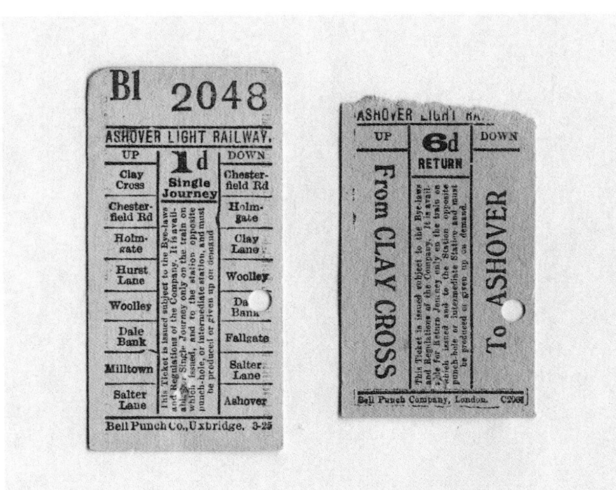

Chapter Six

North

EASINGWOLD RAILWAY

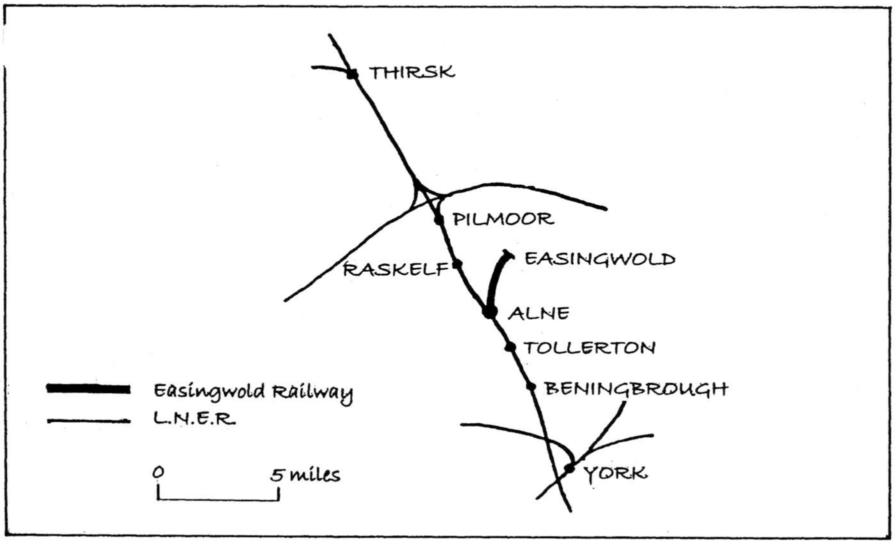

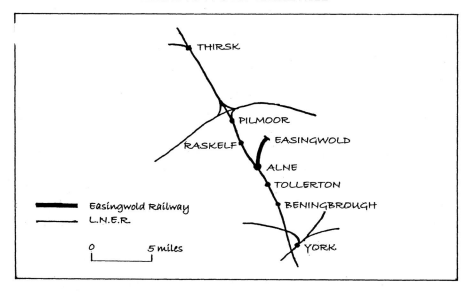

EASINGWOLD and. ALNE. --Easingwold. -- 2½ miles (Time on Journey 8 mins.).
Easingwold to Alne. WEEK DAYS at 7.30, 8.36, 10.25 and 11.2 mrn. ; 1.5, 3.15 and 5 aft.
Alne to Easingwold. WEEK DAYS at 8.10, 9.12, 10.40 and 11.20 mrn. ; 1.38, 3.37 and 5.36 aft.

Figure 6.1 0-6-0ST No.2, Hudswell Clarke no.608 of 1903.

This standard gauge railway, which was 2½ miles long, was opened in 1891 to connect the town of Easingwold with the busy East Coast main line to Scotland. The connection was made at Alne, twelve miles north of York.

When I visited this line at Alne I found the smart-looking 0-6-0ST No.2, built by Hudswell Clarke in 1903, works no.608 (figure 6.1).

All was very quiet at the station and I was ushered into the office where I was presented to the General Manager who granted me permission to take photographs. I remember a distinguished elderly gentleman wearing a stiff upright white collar who looked grand enough to be in charge of a Main Line Railway rather than one whose length was only just over two miles.

The Easingwold Railway ceased carrying passengers in 1948, but continued with goods traffic until 1957 when the railway was finally closed.

RAVENGLASS AND ESKDALE RAILWAY

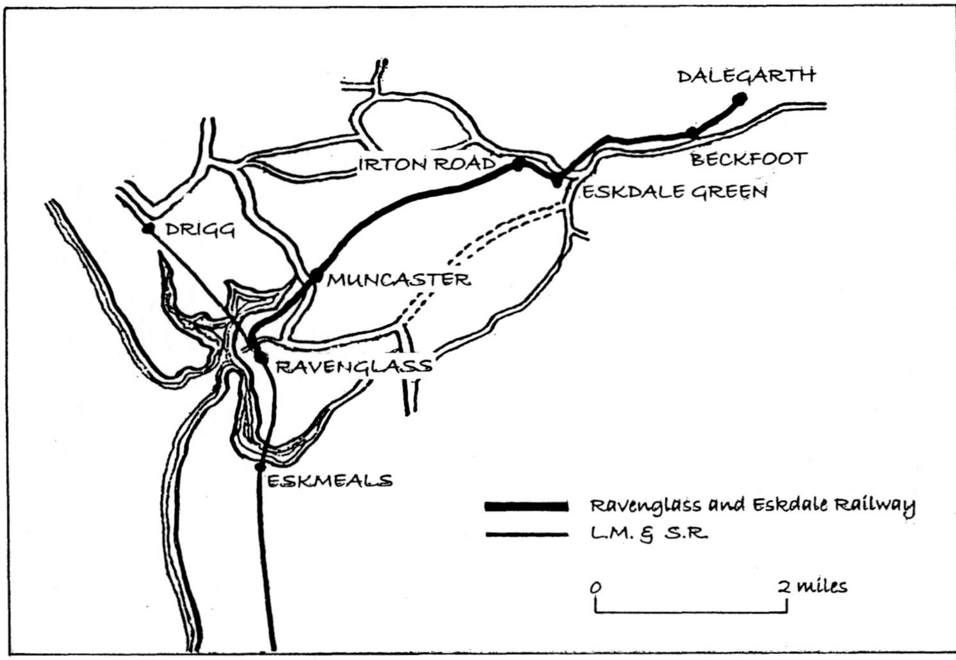

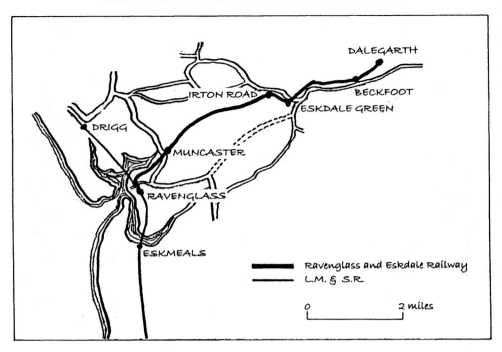

RAVENGLASS, ESKDALE GREEN, and DALEGARTH.—Ravenglass and Eskdale.

Miles	Week Days.	Thurs. only mrn		Sats. only mrn		mrn		aft	aft	Sats. only aft	aft		Sundays. mrn		aft				
	Ravenglass............dep.	7 20	..	9 25	..	1115	..	1 0	3 10	4 20	6 50	..	1145	..	2 30	..	..	..	..
4¼	Irton Road..............	7 40	..	9 45	..	1135	..	1 20	3 30	4 40	7 10	..	1210	..	2 50	..	..	..	..
5	Eskdale Green..............	7 45	..	9 50	..	1140	..	1 25	3 35	4 45	7 15	..	1215	..	2 55	..	..	..	..
6½	Beckfoot **Z**..............	7 55	..	10 5	..	1155	..	1 40	3 50	4 55	7 25	..	1230	..	3 10	..	..	..	..
7	**Dalegarth**.............arr.	8 0	..	1010	..	12 0	..	1 45	3 55	5 0	7 30	..	1235	..	3 15	..	..	..	..

Miles	Week Days.	Thurs. only mrn		Sats. only mrn		aft	aft		aft	aft				Sundays. aft		aft		aft		
	Dalegarth.............,.dep.	8 5	..	1015	..	12 5	2 15	..	5 5	8 0	..	..	..	1245	..	5 5	..	7 0	..	..
½	Beckfoot **Y**..............	8 7	..	1020	..	12 7	2 17	..	5 7	8 2	..	..	..	1247	..	5 7	..	7 2	..	..
2	Eskdale Green..............	8 15	..	1030	..	1215	2 25	..	5 15	8 10	..	..	..	1255	..	5 15	..	7 10	..	..
2¾	Irton Road..............	8 20	..	1035	..	1220	2 30	..	5 20	8 15	..	..	..	1 0	..	5 20	..	7 15	..	..
7	**Ravenglass 618, 620**....arr.	8 45	..	11 0	..	1240	2 50	..	5 40	8 40	..	..	..	1 20	..	5 40	..	7 40	..	..

Y Stop to take up. **Z** Stop to set down.

The Ravenglass and Eskdale Railway, which opened in 1875, was the first narrow gauge public railway in England, and ran for seven miles from Ravenglass on the coast of the Lake District up into the fells. Two special 3ft gauge steam locomotives were designed for this line by Manning Wardle.

After the steady decline of the iron-ore mines on which the railway depended, the line was closed in 1913 to both goods and passengers.

After two years, it was reopened, having been altered to 15in gauge. The first engines were small, some of scale-model type. The heavy work at Beckfoot Quarry, to which there was no road access, was too much for these small engines, and very much larger ones were developed.

During my visit to Ravenglass I saw three large interesting locomotives (figure 6.2). They were 2-8-2 *River Esk* (figure 6.3), 0-8-2 *River Irt* and 4-6-0-0-6-4 *River Mite*.

Figure 6.2 Three locomotives in the shed.

Figure 6.3 2-8-2 *River Esk*, built by Davey Paxman in 1923.

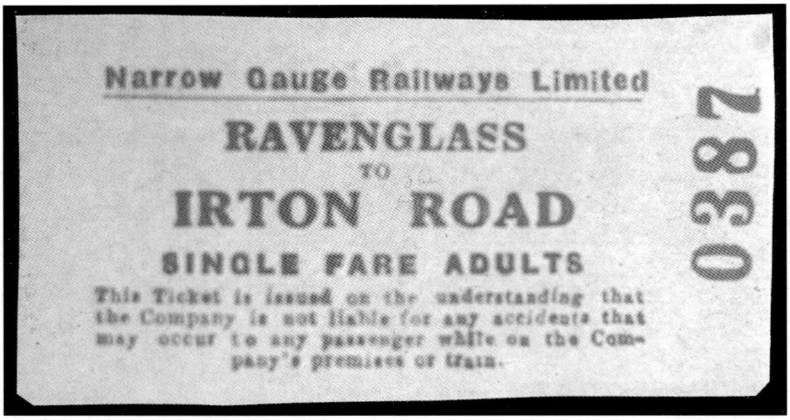

Ravenglass & Eskdale ticket.

Afterthoughts

I visited and photographed twenty-four independent light railways, but there had been twenty-five on my original list of 1931. The missing one was the North Sunderland Light Railway. The reason is simply that it was too far north and could not be fitted in with a visit to any other railway. Nevertheless the map and the timetable were prepared.

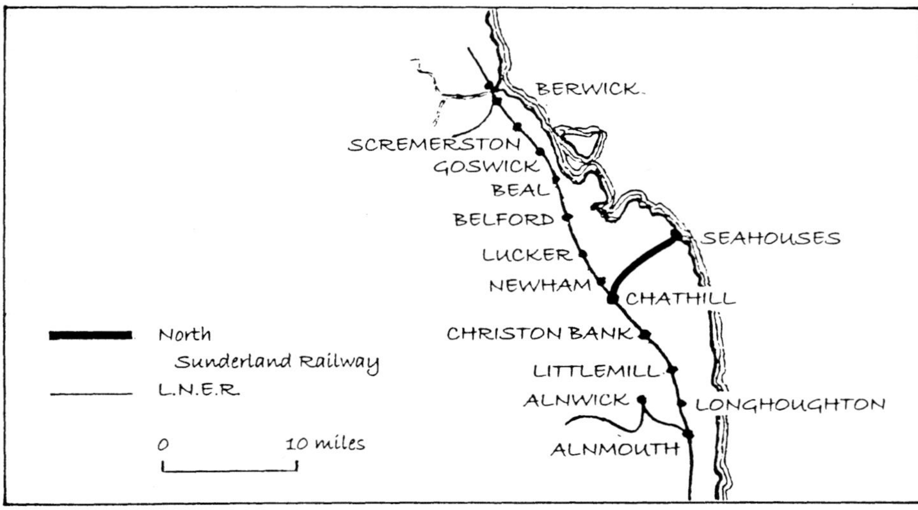

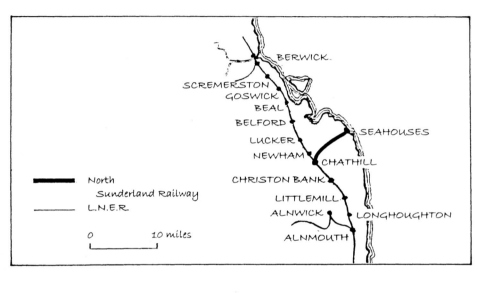

CHATHILL and SEAHOUSES.—North Sunderland.—4 miles. (Time on Journey 15 mins.).
Chathill to Seahouses. WEEK DAYS at 8 12 and 10 48 mrn.; 12 42 Sats., 2, 5 42, and 7 5 aft.
Seahouses to Chathill. WEEK DAYS at 7 48 and 9 20 mrn.; 12 10 Sats., 1 10, 4 10, and 6 30 aft.

Map and timetable prepared for visiting the North Sunderland Railway

This standard gauge line was just over four miles long and was opened in 1898 from Chathill on the L.N.E.R. main line to the town of Seahouses on the coast. There was one named engine and three carriages. I discovered later that the engine was *Bamburgh*, a Manning Wardle 0-6-0ST, no.1394 of 1898, but that it was scrapped in 1949, two years before the railway closed.

Another interesting railway that I just missed was the 3ft gauge Southwold Railway in Suffolk on the East Coast. This was closed in 1929, and so did not feature on my list. However I heard that six years after closure the locomotives were still stored in the shed. At this time I was learning to fly at Cambridge, so I arranged to take my cross-country navigation test from Cambridge to Southwold and back. Flying the Club's Gypsy Moth, I found my way to Southwold and duly circled above the shed - unfortunately the doors were closed and I sadly returned to Cambridge.

Many of the railways I visited and the locomotives I photographed have now completely disappeared. However it is good to know that a few railways have been saved from extinction by enthusiasts, and that some of the locomotives I photographed over sixty years ago are still operating.